Adam

You Are Descended from Adam!
What about Adam?

R. C. Besteder

WESTBOW
PRESS®
A DIVISION OF THOMAS NELSON
& ZONDERVAN

WestBow Press books may be ordered through booksellers or by contacting:

WestBow Press
A Division of Thomas Nelson & Zondervan
1663 Liberty Drive
Bloomington, IN 47403
www.westbowpress.com
1 (866) 928-1240

Because of the dynamic nature of the Internet, any web addresses or links contained in this book may have changed since publication and may no longer be valid. The views expressed in this work are solely those of the author and do not necessarily reflect the views of the publisher, and the publisher hereby disclaims any responsibility for them.

Photo Credit to Corey Besteder

ISBN: 978-1-4497-9851-2 (sc)
ISBN: 978-1-4497-9850-5 (e)

Print information available on the last page.

WestBow Press rev. date: 03/02/2017

Contents

The Sorrow of Adam and Eve

Introduction

Adam was the first human, man on planet earth. Since we are all descended from Adam, every person ought to be interested in knowing about him. Knowledge of Adam gives every individual dignity, significance, and purpose. It helps us to understand why each of us has tremendous potential. The story of Adam gives us hope, a desire to take care of our planet, and a reason to be at peace with all the people of our world.

Our resource on Adam is the Bible. Much of Western society looks to venerable Greek culture for foundations in history, dismissing the Scripture as full of myths. Yet the Greeks saturated their writings with mythical beings, gods, from who men have descended (Herodotus),[1] winged serpents (Herodotus),[2] and many other obvious fabrications, like a giant bird that rises from ashes (the phoenix) or a horse that flies (Pegasus), plus much more.

Just suppose an ancient resource was found that provided valuable insight and truth about our beginning. Such a discovery would be phenomenal and would be great news everywhere throughout the world. We, of course, have it and have had it all along. It predates the Greek culture of 500 BC. Archeology has proved its historicity over and over.[3] The Psalms and Proverbs in it, which also predate Herodotus, who is designated as the father of history, are without a doubt the most beautiful and meditative writings that can be found not only in ancient literature but also in our

---

1   Translated by George Rawlinson, *The History of Herodotus*. (Chicago: The Great Books, by Encyclopaedia Britannica Inc., 1988), 80.

2   Ibid., 113.

3   To see how archeology proves biblical data to be true time and time again, read through the *Archaeological Study Bible*. (Grand Rapids, MI: Zondervan, 2005).

own time. Giving the Bible a fair consideration, it must be admitted one really can't know what the Bible records on Adam until one examines it. And that's what this book is about. Proverbs 18:13 is appropriate: "He who answers a matter before he hears it, It is folly and shame to him."

I think I am equipped to give a good exegesis on Adam, having been schooled in the Scripture through a number of educational institutions at a collegiate and graduate level. I have pastored churches, served as a USAF chaplain for twenty-one years, and have studied the Bible, Genesis through Revelation once a year, in numerous versions, over decades. My purpose is to elicit the incredible body of information about Adam found in the Scripture and to expound on the relevance of Adam as extolled in the message of the Bible itself.

Many Christians have been taught from information in the Bible that Adam was the first man, but they know little about him. Even most pastors or priests who teach the Scripture and folk in Christian educational pursuits spend little time studying about Adam or teaching about him. Some may think of him as a primitive, one stage earlier than a nut gatherer or a cave dweller. Such could not be further from the truth. In fact, earth's people, for the most part, do not think seriously about Adam.

Most Christians know of Adam as the first man but have spent little time contemplating how he fits into the general scheme of things as it relates to man or it meshes with the way volumes of cheap world histories present prehistory. If Adam was the first human being on earth, created by God as a perfect being, how does that relate to us in our modern time, and is there any message in it for us today?

In Western history, Adam was always recognized as an actual factual man, not a mythical being or some kind of allegory. Genesis, contextually, in the Bible does not present him as some kind of literary device representative of the human race. Through sermons, theology, and literature, for thousands of years, Adam was understood to be a literal individual. Recently, as an example, David McCullough, in his Pulitzer Prize–winning book *Truman*, wrote our thirty-third president was instructed that "the panorama of history ... began with Adam and Eve."[4] McCullough didn't write to prove Adam was the first person in history but to present the background under which Harry S. Truman was educated. Millions and millions of other Christians worldwide— Roman Catholics, Protestants, Greek Orthodox, and others—were taught the same.

In addition, salvation history in the Bible is not usually associated with Adam. It is clear, though, that God's program for people to live forever with Him in a celestial place of glory is through faith. It has always been so. God's heroes of faith unquestionably began with Abel, the son of Adam, as referenced in Hebrews 11:4. Enoch was second in verse 5 and Noah third in verse 7. No disrespect to Abraham and not to take anything away from the covenant God made with him or God's intent through him, but salvation history does not begin with him. Great men of God like Jonathan Edwards, a notable philosopher, preacher, author, and past president of Princeton University, taught that our first parents, Adam and Eve, were saved by faith.[5]

There is a veritable wealth of relevant providential data available on Adam that touches every aspect of our lives, including the core issue pertaining to life which is our vital need for our continued existence. Winston Churchill used to say, "You cannot understand the present unless you understand the past." To get oriented, go back to the beginning. This book, *Adam*, contains fifty chapters. How can that be? In Adam's story, we have the beginning of planet earth, the creation of man, the institution of the family, what a family is, what it means to be a husband and have a wife and children, sexuality, spirituality, the first murder, capital punishment, and a host of other subjects.

---

4   David McCullough, *Truman*. (New York, Simon & Schuster Paperbacks, 1992), 59.

5   Jonathan Edwards, *Jonathan Edwards on Knowing Christ*. (Carlisle, PA: The Banner of Truth Trust, Reprinted 1995), 58.

Psychologists have available phenomenal case study on human behavior through analyzing the Scripture on Adam's fall and its results. Contemporary understanding on human behavior from psychology also provides fascinating insight on the saga of Adam and Eve in Genesis, the first book of the Bible. Such study confirms what we have discovered about ourselves and human nature, thus affirming the reality and truthfulness of our resource.

The elucidation in *Adam* covers many topics but is not expansive or all inclusive. There is no claim here to have exhausted the topic or what may be known about Adam. The chapters for the most part are short by design so the book is an easy read and fast moving. Emphasis is placed on simplicity to abet comprehension.

Hopefully readers will find the material in this book intellectually and spiritually stimulating, a pleasant surprise, and serendipity, and it will lead to a renewed interest in what is to be found in a thorough study of Scripture, treasures often glossed over, forgotten, or ignored. An example is the insight on the way God set up our calendar, hence the keeping of time. Another is the age of Adam itself and the fact that it is recorded in the book of Genesis. The chapters on the intellect of Adam and the stature of Adam are not for debate but for matters of interest on him as a perfect man, a phenomenal human being.

A reemphasis on the reality and significance of Adam is timely. As we take another look at him, we are awed at what we discover and how biblical teaching on him is not only up to date and highly enlightening but also gives transport by the Second Adam into the ages to come.

Scriptures quoted in the text are from the New King James Version of the Bible, unless otherwise referenced. Scriptures used in the text which are not quoted or containing a phrase from the New King James Version of the Bible may be read from any version of the Bible. In addition, it may be of interest to readers to know that I have been interested in the subject of Adam since my youth, especially following the influence of my confirmation. My passion for this venue continued through a spiritual birth, my scriptural Christian education, various ministerial experiences, and the sojourn of my life. My enthusiasm on the theme of Adam, and hence an interest and love for all mankind and world history, led me to inquisitive reading in many of the resources, supporting documents, and established facts referenced in this book. I genuinely believe God has guided me in my thought processes on the subject of Adam through many years of study and that He has given me the illumination to write this book.

Adam—a Composition

Luminosity radiated from his lithe, athletic body as he lay peacefully sleeping, basking in the mid-afternoon sun. Slowly his eyes opened, and he gazed into the crystal blue heavens, reflecting on the majesty of the one who had breathed into him the breath of life. Again he thought about his name—Adam, Adam from the ground. He knew he was made from the earth. And a wondrous earth it was. He sat up and looked around at the beautiful flowers—color delighted his eyes from everywhere. A gentle breeze rippled through the grass so that it seemed to be waving to him, and the rustle of leaves in the trees reminded him that the spirit of the Creator was present. Multifarious greens sparkled from plant life enhanced by the glorious brilliance of the sun.

Gracefully he stood and walked to a nearby fount of artesian water shooting up twelve feet, just even with his lips. He drank. It was cool and refreshing.

Walking a few yards, he reached upward, fifteen feet, and picked a fruit. It was juicy and delicious. After eating some other varieties of fruit, he made his way to his favorite tree, which Elohim called the Tree of Life. He picked only one piece and ate. As always, he felt life surging through his being—a power burst. Adam laughed. He glowed. He started to run. Moving faster than the speed of cheetah, he glided through grassy meadows toward the great river on his left. Animals were everywhere watching him; some running with him—jumping and frolicking. They loved Adam.

Adam jumped on the back of one running just ahead. His mount said, "Thank you for choosing me today, Master Adam. Why do you ride me when you run faster than me?"

"Ah," said Adam, "I honor you because next to the serpent, you are the most beautiful creature in the garden."

"Thank you," said Leviathan. "Indeed, I am greatly honored."

1

The First Man

Adam—Hebrew for red, earthly, taken out of the red earth—was the first human being on planet earth.[6] We know this truth from a written record that is foundational for a major portion of the world's population—namely the Christian, Jewish, and Muslim people.[7] Out of the area where these people lived—the Near East, Egypt, Greece, and Rome—written records were developed that became the science and art of history. History of course contains records from all peoples and includes all peoples of our world.

History properly begins with Adam. All people of planet earth are descended from Adam—red, yellow, black, and white. The first man, Adam, carried in his seed what would become the human race as we now know it. Our resource, however, does not identify people according to color. It presents all human life generically, as "man," the human race, mankind.[8]

---

6   Merril F. Unger, *Unger's Bible Dictionary*. (Chicago, Moody Press, 1970) 19. John Farrar, *People and Places in the Bible*. (Westwood, NJ: Barbour Books, 1987), 11.

7   The Old Testament creation account in the Bible with Adam as the first man has been traditional in the Christian and Jewish faiths and also is accepted by Muslims.

8   In Job 5:7 ,an Old Testament biblical passage, the term *man* is used in a generic way: "Yet man is born to trouble, As the sparks fly upward."

Recognizing Adam as the first man orients all people in our world toward a solid relational basis. It correctly directs us philosophically, practically, and politically to the focus we all know in our hearts is true, and that is there is really only one race on planet earth—the human race. This gives insight into a major problem: racism.

In the United States, many contemporary historians write and teach about the invasion of North America by white people from Europe. The cause of deep racism against Native Americans and African Americans is attributed to white people. The United States in particular is singled out as an evil nation. In such a treatment, other world histories—ancient, through the ages, and contemporary—are ignored. The flames of racism are kept burning, especially by white intellectuals who cannot get over the past and in particular many of their own personally imposed hurdles.

It is a breath of fresh air to know Adam is the parent of us all. Man's inhumanity to man is not limited to the United States. It is a condition man suffers due to his alienation from his Creator. Racism began with cultural and physiological differences developed through the centuries as mankind spread over the face of the earth. It continued through greed and lasciviousness as those who had power used it to enslave others. One of the greatest abusers of mankind was the Roman Empire. Its slavery, however, was not based on race. Slavery itself leads to racism. Such has been particularly true in the United States.

Racism is further perpetuated by sociological studies, so-called sciences that divide people into groups. It is furthered by politicians who keep it going to secure political power and carry out political goals.

It is interesting to me that some never tire of talking about the horrors of things done to people of color. I do remember, unless I am deceiving myself, that I learned as a chaplain in the US Air Force in social actions on race relations—an equal-opportunity undertaking—that all people are people of color. Is it too simple to say that all people are people?

Any person who studies history knows that through the ages worldwide, all kinds of horrific things have been done to others, in many cases to people of other cultures or to people who are not of the same group. There is evil in the world, and it is not confined to any one period in world history, to any one culture, to any one race, to any one group or tribe, to any one nation, to any one family, or to any one individual.

However, we the people of the world are all one in Adam. He is our biological father. It is time for the people of our planet to move beyond racism. We know it is wrong and there is no excuse for it. Nor is there any excuse to follow people who perpetuate it. What should we say about it? It is important to study history, noting our failures as well as the good. Let's strive for a balanced treatment of the truth and at the same time get past hatred, discrimination, and demagoguery by having the individual courage, with educators, politicians, peers at work, family members, and friends, to say, "Stop it!" to racist language and behavior.

There is much we can learn from Adam, the first man. Knowing about Adam orients us, clarifies our history, and is highly enlightening. It will lead us to decisions that will be helpful to others and satisfying for ourselves. It can secure for us endless life. It should connect us, if we are not already connected, to our source of life, happiness, and power—our Creator.

Furthermore, those who claim to have a religious faith with teachings significantly attached to Adam through our resource need to become consistent in their belief. Elijah at Mount Carmel, in a time of religious confusion, called the people of Israel to a firm stand for their God. He cried out, "How long will you falter between two opinions? If the Lord is God follow Him" (1 Kings 18:21).[9] If you claim to be a Christian or a Jew, the historic teaching has been and still is that Adam, Adam of the Bible, was the first man. Adam was an actual factual human. What about Adam?

---

9   In 1 Kings 18 Elijah, one of the greatest prophets in the Old Testament, challenged King Ahab of Israel to a contest between God and the prophets of Baal on Mount Carmel. Israel at that time was in violation of the first two of the Ten Commandments listed in Exodus 20.

2

Created

Adam, the titular head of the human race, had no bellybutton. "The Lord God formed man of the dust of the ground and breathed into his nostrils the breath of life, and man became a living being [soul]" (Gen. 2:7). Adam did not walk with a stoop; he walked with God. Man did not begin as a primate. He was created—a perfect being. Man did not accidentally ascend. From Adam man retrogressed. This explains why archeologists and historians are astounded by the mathematical skills and precision in early civilization found in the remains of the Egyptian pyramids, the astronomical knowledge of the Babylonians, or the heating and cooling facilities of the Minoans.

Adam lived in a garden paradise. "The Lord God planted a garden eastward in Eden [from a word meaning delight], and there he put the man whom he had formed" (Gen. 2:8). Adam did not live in a cave. He didn't need a house or a tent. Climatic conditions were controlled by God with Eden's thermostat. It was not too cold or too hot. Adam didn't need a coat or even clothes, for that matter. He didn't need a closet. Adam didn't need a mall he could regularly visit to buy an abundance of things. He had no things. Adam did not have anything, yet Adam had everything. All was Adam's.

Downgraded from Adam significantly, shortly after the flood, in the days of Peleg, the fifteenth generation from Adam (see Gen. 10:25), people separated and began to wander over planet earth. One grouping of those who scattered, Native Americans, migrated to North America, becoming the first settlers. Retaining some knowledge of their original home after the flood and the inhabitants who lived with them before they left, they referred to themselves as "the People." In their manner of living, they were more like Adam in the garden than the settlers who came from Europe. And indeed, Native Americans are the People. All of us are the People, descendants of Adam, made by the Creator. All people originally knew this truth.

Adam could sleep wherever he wanted in perfect comfort and peace. No creature would hurt him. In fact, Adam was the master of the garden. "The Lord God took the man and put him in the garden of Eden to tend and keep it" (Gen. 2:15). All the creatures of the garden knew Adam, respected him, and all were under his supervision.

> Out of the ground the Lord God formed every beast of the field and every bird of the air and brought them to Adam to see what he would name them. And whatever Adam called each living creature was its name. So Adam gave names to all cattle, to the birds of the air, and to every beast of the field [including behemoth and Leviathan—Job 40–41]. (Gen. 2:19–20)

Adam did not kill animals. I am not proposing we should eat no meat. Mankind began to eat meat in the days of Noah, after the flood (see Gen. 9:1–3). What I am noting is that it was not the practice of Adam in the garden to eat animals. "Out of the garden the Lord God made every tree grow that is pleasant to the sight and good for food." (Gen. 2:9). And the Lord God commanded the man, "Of every tree of the garden you may freely eat" (Gen. 2:16). (There was one exception. Adam was strictly forbidden not to eat of the Tree of the Knowledge of Good and Evil in the middle of the garden – Genesis 2:17.) Adam's food consisted of vegetables and fruit.

Adam's original morality concerning animals was retained in the memory of people living in India, who incorporated it into their religious practices.

It also influenced Native Americans, who for the most part never killed more than they could eat or use. Observe when the Native American Chingachgook in the movie *The Last of the Mohicans* apologized to a deer for taking its life. Native Americans knew all life was sacred. Adam was the caretaker, under the Lord God, to planet earth. Adam was a lover of animals and cared for creatures.

Adam did not need protection from the rain. It did not rain in Adam's lifetime. Initially God did not cause it to rain on the earth (Gen. 2:5). "A mist went up from the earth and watered the whole face of the ground" (Gen. 2:6).

Adam had no use for an automobile, a train, an airplane, or even a horse. He didn't need to go anywhere. Everything he needed was at his fingertips. Adam had all kinds of fruit, trees, and plants in his garden, animals galore, and a river to water it (Gen. 2:10–14). Obviously Adam had many streams and fountains, and best of all, he had fellowship with his Creator. God walked in the garden and could be heard doing so. He talked with Adam. See Genesis 3:8.

3

God's Image

Pursuant to understanding what it means to be created in the image of God, it is vital to comprehend the essence of what Adam was. Our resource, the Scripture, teaches Genesis 2:7, "And the Lord God formed man of the dust of the ground and breathed into his nostrils the breath of life and man became a living being [soul]."

The Hebrew word for being is *nephesh*. God did not give Adam a soul. The soul is not a vestige in one's body. The first man was a living soul, a nephesh.

So what is a nephesh, a living soul? Genesis 2:7 teaches that Adam was made of the earth—that is, he was physical. But Adam was also a living "being." What made Adam a being, a *bios* (a Greek word for life), was the *ruah* put into him by the Spirit of God (the Hebrew word for breath or spirit is ruah). Adam, or man, is more than material. Yes, we are made of the elements of the earth, but we are beings, spiritually endowed, novel creatures. Adam individually and specifically was a sensational, specialized, living being placed on planet earth. As a man, Adam was flesh and blood, chemically of the dust, but he, living and operating by the breath of God, was a godlike spirit. The man, Adam—as a body and a spirit in that body—was created a living soul. Early man knew this truth. For instance, the Native Americans, retaining this ancient knowledge, knew a man was a spirit and the Creator was the Great Spirit.

Animals were also created living souls. In Genesis 1:24 God created the living creature or living souls—nephesh. All creatures are living souls. The difference, however, between an animal and a man is that an animal is not made in the image of God. Adam was created in the image of God. Genesis 1:26 records, "Let us make man in our image, after our likeness," which means man is made in the likeness of God. The Hebrew word for likeness, *demut*, which means "similar," simply indicates we are like God. It tells us about our "image. Man, male and female, was created by God to be like God.

At first there was only male. Later God created the female. But both male and female, by divine design, the creative act of Almighty God, are in the image of God (Gen. 1:27). This does not mean God is an anthropomorphic being having arms and legs or a body like a human. We are made in God's image; He is not made in ours. God's image is not physical, although God gave dignity to the way He made Adam physically, in that Adam did not walk with a stoop or swing from trees. Mankind walks upright. Man acts with dignity or at least was created to conduct himself in a dignified way.

Man is male and female. God is neither. Repeatedly, the image of God is not physical; God does not have male or female genitals. God is Spirit (John 4:24). To be made, then, in God's image is to be made in God's likeness, to be essentially a godlike spirit.

Further, man is a spirit with moral consciousness, having the freedom of choice. It means we are unique beings in the universe identified by our ability to love, artistic beauty, intelligence, awareness of self, sense of worth, creativity, and spirituality. Examining people's activity in world history, we can see and greatly appreciate all these facets of God's image in us. They do not mean we are God or that we will be gods, but in them we acknowledge revelatory Spirit input about

Adam

Adam and the image of God. We as descendants of Adam, Adam's children, are like God—in His image, atypical, special, and distinct in creation.

It is indispensable to the psychology of man—our understanding of who we are—to emphasize we are made in God's image and to know what that means. Such knowledge compels us to treat each other with reverence and respect. Adam was made in God's image and for fellowship or interaction with others. He was created in God's image for relationship with God Himself. God made us relational. The most significant aspect of God's image in us has to do with our relationships. In them God made us to bless self and others. For man God made everything beautiful in its time. Life on earth is supposed to be enjoyed, with God, as life is in the heavens or celestial realms (Eccl. 2:24).

For our most significant actualization, we are cognizant that when God made us in His image, He put eternity in our hearts (Eccl. 3:11). It is for that reason that all mankind according to our earliest written records has been religious. Mankind has an innate desire to know God and to worship him. Mankind, in all civilizations, has believed in an afterlife and has hoped after their life on planet earth that they would be with God in a better place. Without revelation, the specifics of our earliest resource on Adam, mankind has only obscure memories of the beginning and these truths.

To be mentally well people were made for a vertical relationship (i.e., with God) and healthy intimate relationships with others (horizontal interrelatedness). It was so from the beginning. It was not good for Adam to be alone, just to have animals for a relationship, although some animals do provide wonderful friendship, so God made "Eve," a woman (Gen. 2:18–25). God instituted the family for the good of Adam and the good of Eve as well. Society began with a family. Adam's vertical relationship with God and the horizontal relationship God established between Adam and his wife, or for one human with another, is a reflection of the image of God.

Furthermore, on the image of God, God made every human with tremendous potential. From Adam to men in our time, all mankind has been the same, capable of individual and corporate feats that seem impossible.

Know, in addition, that God also did not purpose for mankind to continue in a physical state forever on planet earth. It becomes clear as God's history of man progresses in our resource called revelation that man was to be like God in a celestial realm. "As we have borne the image of the man of dust, we shall also bear the image of the heavenly Man" (1 Cor. 15:49). Again this does not mean a man will become a god. It does mean man, Adam, was made with the intention of being with God in His celestial realm in the heavens. There a person's existence will be different. The preciousness of family life here metaphorically points to a preferable and glorious life with God as His family forever.

4

Photographic Memory

Remember, Adam was created a perfect man. It's not a stretch to know he had a photographic memory. A major obstacle to understanding Adam is not being able to relate to the environment in which he lived. To accomplish any kind of realistic study on Adam, one must mentally consider him from the perspective we are furnished by our resource. It is difficult to do so because of the mountains of subterfuge presenting man as a mere chance happening and all that accompanies that approach.

Adam did not need fire. He did not need a wheel or a horse. Adam did not have a radio, a telephone, a television, a computer, a phonograph, or even a book, for that matter. In the last hundred years, knowledge has exploded so vastly that it's hard to even begin to comprehend what Adam's life was like.

Psychologists tell us we use a small portion of our brains and we are capable of much greater mental feats. We are told some among us have great memories—photographic memories. I'm not sure what that means except that some people are mentally equipped to impress us with almost total recall.

Kim Peek, about whom a movie was made entitled *Rain Man*, starring Dustin Hoffman, was one such a man. He could read two pages in a book at the same time, the left page with his left eye and the right page with his right eye, in eight seconds with 98 percent recall.[10]

People like Peek are called savant, having special knowledge in a specific area. Daniel Tammet from Great Britain had a series of seizures that did something to his brain. When asked under examination to square pi, he did so to the twenty-two thousandth, giving 514 digits in five hours and nine minutes. When later examined by other scientists he was able to give the square of any number far beyond the digits on a calculator. As a special test, he went to Iceland and learned the Icelandic language, the most difficult in the world, in one week. He spoke the Icelandic language perfectly in a nationally televised documentary, astounding the people of that country.[11] Tammet and others like him are able to give knowledge of which day of the week, Sunday through Saturday, any date of a month in a specific year occurred, what the weather was like on that day, and many other documented correct particulars.

Peek and Tammet are used by psychologists to prove scientifically that we only use small portions of our brains. Tammet's ability and others like him are inexplicable. Trying to be scientific, it is said their extraordinary mental ability is attributed to areas of the brain unused by modern man. My understanding is those who do such things inherit it from someone who went before them.[12] Adam of course was our original prototype. The first man, who was perfect, used his total brain.

We are told that there are people of the Islamic faith who memorize the entire Qur'an. The Qur'an is smaller than the Bible and is supposed to be

---

10 Yahoo, Kim Peek Reference Articles. Find Target Reference. *Early Life*. 1.

11 Yahoo, Daniel Tammet Reference Articles. Find Target Reference. *PI, Language Abilities*. 1–2.

12 Yahoo, Genetics—Inherited Intelligence. *The Role of Genetics in IQ and Intelligence*. A to Z of Brain, Mind, and Learning: "Your brain … is constructed according to instructions received from the genes that you have inherited from your parents," 1.

easier to memorize. I have read it, and it is a good-size book. To memorize the Qur'an, seems to me, would be an impressive accomplishment.

I had an airman friend in the air force who claimed he had thirteen books of the New Testament memorized. He is a man of integrity. I never asked him to repeat them to me, but I believe he could awe us, as some can with biblical quotations. We could go on and on demonstrating people's ability to retain knowledge, whether it is professional singers, theatrical performers, gifted academic professors, sports fans with a bent for trivia, or whatever. The point related to Adam, a perfect man, is that he was created with a superior intellect and a super-human memory.

I knew a chaplain in the air force who could go to a social luncheon, be introduced to thirty people, and after lunch, when it came time to leave, shake every individual's hand speaking to each person by name. Adam could do it.

> Out of the ground the Lord God formed every beast of the field and every bird of the air and brought them to Adam to see what he would call them. And whatever Adam called each living creature that was its name. So Adam gave names to all the cattle, to the birds of the air, and to every beast of the field. (Gen. 2:19–20)

Adam, caretaker of planet earth, named every living creature on it. Adam certainly gave names to plant life as well. Adam was the first biologist. We don't know all he knew. But we do know he didn't have to write it in a book or put it into a computer. It was all in his head, and he had total recall.

I've been taught that we inherit our abilities and traits from those from whom we descend. This being so the first generations of humankind on our planet were far superior intellectually to those we study in written secular history and to our current residents. Using longevity as a measuring stick (Adam lived to be 930 years—Gen. 5:5), we can ascertain that mankind slowly, over the years since creation, after what we call the Fall, diminished not only in the length of life span but also in stature and intellectual capacity, subjects we will address in later chapters.

Some who study early man from a biblical perspective insist there must have been early written records. Maybe there were. The question is why would there be such records? Adam and his descendants for many generations did not need them. Adam established history through oral tradition.

I went to Emmanuel Christian Seminary in Johnson City, Tennessee, specifically because Dr. Toyozo W. Nakarai taught there. An eminent Hebrew scholar who used his own textbook, *Biblical Hebrew*, Nakarai was listed in the Who's Who in the World, Who's Who in America, and Who's Who in Religion.[13] A remarkable man, Nakarai was a physical relative of the emperor of Japan—a samurai warrior who fought before the emperor, winning the contest among swordsmen. Nakarai knew Shintoism and Buddhism. He taught Japanese and Chinese history in Japan before his conversion to Christianity.

When he came to the United States, Nakarai taught the Japanese language and literature at the College of Missions in Indiana. An author, a scholar, and an ordained minister, he held distinguished professorships teaching the Old Testament at Butler, Indiana, and at Emmanuel Christian Seminary in Johnson City, Tennessee. I remember him teaching that our knowledge in the early chapters of Genesis the first book of the Bible came from oral tradition. He knew what he was talking about. Not only did he understand Adam and the early generations of mankind from his scholarly study, but his cultural background also provided him with additional comprehension. Much of what he knew, and earlier generations of scholars knew, has been lost and obscured by a lack of understanding about how early people passed on knowledge.

---

13 Toyozo W. Nakarai, *Biblical Hebrew* (Philadelphia, PA: Bookman Associates, Inc., 1951), vii–x.

When I was a boy, I can remember regular visits to elderly neighbors, on their front porch, listening to them talk about past generations of their families. People rarely do that anymore, especially here in the United States. In the past, it was important for a family to pass on to posterity knowledge about themselves and their folks.

The record of the creation and Adam, plus his succeeding generations, was not lost. It was important to those who lived the early life of mankind according to the grand scheme of things to accurately preserve what happened. The Creator Himself who gave life to Adam and providentially is orchestrating His purpose for mankind made sure all has been reliably retained. If God could create our planet, it would be easy for Him to document His work, first through oral tradition and then in a written record. Understand, the writing of Scripture is not millions of years old.

Dr. Philip Schaff, a brilliant historian, writes in his *History of the Christian Church*, volume 1, "History has two sides, a divine and a human."[14] Our resource on Adam, though written by a man, is a divinely inspired history.

The history of man, a written history, didn't begin until mankind could no longer do business through his intellectual prowess. Earlier Adam, who didn't have the distractions we do today, in a setting conducive to concentration and focus, with a superior intellect, operated by memory. This evidently was true for generations after Adam. The first generations of mankind would be greatly amused at our modus operandi. They had no newspapers, magazines, books, or writings of any kind. If we could time travel back to Adam's world, it would be more of a shock to us than our modern world would be to him. That's why at the Tower of Babel, after the flood, God scattered people over the world and gave them different languages. If He had not done so, it would not have been long before mankind would have been busily engaged with space travel (see Gen. 11:1–9).

---

14 Phillip Schaff, *Volume I History of the Christian Church*. (Grand Rapids, MI: Eerdmans Printing Company, 1910), 20.

5

A Monotheist

Adam was a monotheist. Polytheism came later. Adam is described in the garden as having a relationship with God. When God breathed into Adam the breath of life, Adam's life began. In Adam's first conscious moment, there was God.

When an attempt was made to tell Helen Keller about God, her reply was that she already knew. Adam, I take it, came to consciousness, and he knew God. Adam related to his Father, the personage from whom he came. There was a filial linkage. There still is.

Every human has an empty spot, a void in his or her soul that must be filled. When the void is not filled by the one who made us, we are not at one with our environment, not whole, not the personage we were designed to be. We were made to worship.

When mankind is estranged from God, there is an attempt to fill the void in our lives. After the fall and Adam's expulsion from Eden, mankind was separated from God. Yet the immediate generations of mankind after Adam knew about the creation. As time went on, fewer and fewer people chose to worship God. After the great flood, it was the same. The need to worship led men to invent their own gods, ones in their own images, suitable to their own interests—hence polytheism.[15]

Our source on Adam—oral tradition—was preserved by the righteous line descending from Adam. From that source, and additional revelation written by the prophets of God over a period of fifteen hundred years, we have one continuous, marvelous, harmonious record orchestrated by God concerning His plan for mankind. Part of that knowledge, in the book of Romans, informs us that somewhere in time mankind ceased to worship the Creator and began to worship the creation (Rom. 1:16–32).

---

15 Consider the supposition that Cain was the father of myths. Evidently Adam, with his son Seth and their descendants, for some generations worshipped God the Creator (Gen. 4:26). Cain, like his younger brother Seth, who lived 912 years (Gen. 5:8), would have lived for many generations. It was only natural for him to establish his own form of worship or religion to keep his people from joining Seth, the successor of Abel. This is what Jeroboam, king of Israel, did with the ten tribes that broke away from Judah as recorded in 1 Kings 12:25–33. To keep the people of his kingdom from returning to worship at the temple in Jerusalem and from offering allegiance to Rehoboam, king of Judah, he made calves of gold and set up counter worship sites at Bethel and Dan. He told the people the calves were the gods that had delivered them out of Egypt (1 Kings 12:28). Wouldn't Cain have done the same? The "way of Cain" (Jude 1:11) was to come up with his own religion. Cain's story would have been to make himself a son of a god, something Adam was, as the Son of God, first created, but something Cain was not.

This, of course, is what we see in the myths. Note, for example, when Virgil, giving us the background of Rome in the *Aeneid*, writes of Aeneas as the son of the goddess Venus. The curse on Cain, a farmer by vocation, meaning the earth would not be fertile for him (Gen. 4:10–13), is much of the reason God's punishment on Cain was greater than he could bear. It also gives a reason for the rise of fertility cults—because of the need to move deity to give a successful harvest. The myths of a god that married his sister is exactly what Cain did. It seems such myths are likely to have originated with Cain. Noah, of course, did not engage in worship that served as an substitute for the true faith, which came through Abel and Seth. But Noah and his sons would have had knowledge of the religious practices started by Cain. Those religious tenets would have been picked up again by Canaan, Ham's son (see Gen. 9:18–27) and have been put to use among the descendants of Canaan in the area of Sodom and also in the Fertile Crescent, where we first read of myths and rulers claiming to be related to deity, representing the gods, in Sumer.

Polytheism is a syncretism of mankind's ideas on God, Satanic in origin. It incorporated the worship of the creation, like the sun and heavenly bodies and the processes of creation, now called nature, into the deification of creation itself. Worshipping the creation is called pantheism. Darwinism is not the first convolution used to nix the true and living God from His own universe. Polytheism did so ages ago. Sarah Iles Johnston notes in *Ancient Religions* "in Greece and Rome, according to the best known cosmologies, neither Zeus/Jupiter nor any other gods creates the world; it simply develops out of chaos on its own."[16]

Polytheism included the deification of men. One reason the gods were concocted was for type-A people to secure power. The earliest written histories record kings claiming to be gods.[17] In the twentieth century, the emperor of Japan claimed descent from the Japanese sun goddess.[18] After World War II, he told the Japanese people he was not a god. Once he relinquished the status of deity, obedience to him was no longer feasible.

We observe polytheism utilized by Virgil in the *Aeneid*. Virgil wrote to exalt Rome, claiming it was founded by Aeneas, whose father was a Trojan hero, Anchises, and whose mother was Venus, the goddess of beauty and erotic love. "The Latins are of Saturn's seed."[19] Virgil of course supported the senate's declaration that Julius Caesar was a god. After Caesar, his nephew, the first Roman emperor, Augustus (the splendid one) was declared a god. Shortly thereafter, the Emperor Caligula, a despicable tyrant, could not wait until after his death for the senate to

---

16 Sarah Iles Johnston, general editor, *Ancient Religion.* (Cambridge, MA: The Belknap Press of Harvard University Press, 2007), 18.

17 Anton Gill, *The Rise and Fall of Babylon, Gateway of the Gods.* (New York: Metro Books, 1908), Naram-Sin, grandson of Sargon of Akkad, 37, Gudea King of Lagash, 38, and Shulgi, King of Ur, 40.

18 Gary D. Allinson, "Chinese Influence," *The World Book Encyclopedia, J-K* (Chicago: A Scott Fetzer Company, 2003), 53.

19 Robert Maynard Hutchins, editor in chief, Virgil, *Great Books of the Western World, 13. Virgil* (Chicago: Encyclopedia Britannica, Inc., 1988), 241.

declare him a god. He had to be a god immediately.[20] Caligula enjoyed letting people know he could have them executed at his least possible whim. After all, he was a god.

Tracing polytheism back in history, we see it existed in the very first civilization of which we have written records. In *World Mythology*, Arthur Cotterell writes, "In ancient Sumer, present day southern Iraq, the oldest surviving myths tell us that kingship' came down from heaven, the ruler being chosen and invested by the assembly of the gods."[21] Going on, "the king was rather like a steward managing the god's estates." Under "Themes of Sumerian Myths," we see the emergence of a coherent cosmic order. In the third dynasty of Ur, the city from which the biblical Abraham originated a number of Sumerian cities was subsumed into one political body. These were "ruled by kings who assumed a quasi-divine status."[22]

A second reason gods were invented was to release mankind from moral restraint. Les Strobel, who wrote *The Case for a Creator*, explains how Darwinism and contemporary teachings on evolution in the 1960s led him to an atheism that gave him freedom from God's moral strictures.[23] Strobel, who later became a Christian, as a journalist par excellence, now writes in favor of the creation. More on this aspect of polytheism will be presented in the chapter on Eve.

A third reason for polytheism is seen in the religions of the Far East. They represent the best effort by humans to rediscover God or to understand the meaning of life. The confusion in all this makes it difficult for many to distinguish fact—the true account of our beginning—from fiction. There is nothing in all these myths or stories even remotely similar to

---

20 Michael Kerrigan, *A Dark History: the Roman Emperors* (New York: Metro Books, 2008), 62, 69–70.

21 Arthur Cotterell, general editor, *World Mythology*. (Bath, UK: Paragon Publishing, 2005), 7–8.

22 Ibid., 15.

23 Lee Strobel, *The Case for a Creator*. (Grand Rapids, MI: Zondervan, 2004), 25.

the story in our resource on Adam. The story of Adam, a divine history, is continuous from the very beginning of mankind, from Adam, to the life of Jesus Christ, only two thousand years ago, and as such is totally unique. Most of those who do not believe it have not read it in its entirety with an honest effort to ascertain whether it is true.

The Hebrew people, by the way, often referred to as the Jews, are given credit for the idea of monotheism. It should be emphasized from our resource on Adam, the Bible, that the Jews did not give us the concept of monotheism.

According to the Bible, Abraham came out of Ur, the myth-laden civilization of the Fertile Crescent (Gen. 11:31). Abraham came from a cultural setting where his father and forefathers knew about God but were caught up in the idolatry of those surrounding them (Josh. 24:2). The God of creation, Adam's God, made a covenant with Abraham, which eventuated in the covenant made with Moses and the people of Israel at Mount Sinai. God was not invented by the Hebrews, those who became the Jews. He always was. It was God that gave the Ten Commandments to the Hebrews in Exodus 20. God communicated, "I am the Lord Your God" and "You shall have no other gods before Me." Monotheism was commanded by God.

The Israelites themselves were continuously in conflict with God, wanting to be like the peoples around them—polytheistic. Ernest G. Wright, a PhD who taught at John Hopkins, in *The Old Testament against Its Environment*, skillfully and adequately demonstrates that Israel did not give us monotheism.[24] They were in covenant with a monotheistic God but never "totally" accepted the concept until after the Babylonian captivity. After they were carried to Babylon and Jerusalem was destroyed in 586 BC, they finally got the idea—proclaim and worship Abraham's God, the true God of the Old Testament, our Creator.

---

24 G. Ernest Wright, *The Old Testament Against Its Environment*. (London, England: SCM Press, 1962), 42–76.

Adam

Mankind, from the beginning, was created to worship the true and living God, Adam's Creator. Adam knew Him. Ancient man knew about Him but as time progressed became more and more estranged from Him. Helen Keller born without sight and without hearing was more aware of the presence of God than most of us who are born with sight and hearing. She knew about God.

Adam never experienced life as a baby or a boy. His consciousness began as a full-grown man. Being created and fellowshipping with God was absolutely wonderful. God spoke to Adam on Adam's first tour of his new home, the garden. Adam received instructions on tending the garden. How exciting it was! It's amazing, but we actually have a small excerpt of what God spoke to Adam: "Of every tree of the garden you may freely eat; but of the tree of the knowledge of good and evil you shall not eat, for in the day that you eat you shall surely die" (Gen. 2:16–17).

Adam adjusted to life in Eden on planet earth. We later learn that no flesh can see God and live. Obviously Adam did not visibly see God in all His glory. But like Enoch, the seventh generation from Adam (Gen. 5:18–24), Adam walked with God. Later in Adam's life, because of his disobedience, or sin, he would be cut off from fellowship with God. However, at the outset of Adam's sojourn on planet earth God made himself accessible to Adam and in the garden Adam had an intimate relationship with God. Since Adam was made perfect he was without sin, both knowing and enjoying the true and living God. And yes, Adam was a monotheist.

6

Monogamous

Adam had one wife. Actually he didn't have a lot of options. If Adam had married again, it would by necessity have been with one of his daughters. Adam had sons and daughters (Gen. 5:4). Because Adam lived many years, 930 (Gen. 5:5), and since Adam's physique was not entirely as ours (more about this later), and because he was commanded to, "Be fruitful and multiply; fill the earth" (Gen. 1:28), Adam had many children. People on earth multiplied rapidly because of the long age span and virility of Adam and his descendants.[25]

It was during Adam's lifetime that men began to have a plurality of wives. Adam's great-grandson three times over, Lamech, took two wives, Adah and Zillah (Gen. 4:19). It was not the intention of God for men to have a plurality of wives. King Solomon, the son of David (killer of the Philistine giant Goliath), had seven hundred wives and three hundred

---

25 Early mankind had rapid demographic growth through the birth of many twins and triplets. It has been suggested that Cain and Abel may have been twins. Jacob and Esau were twins (Gen. 25:21–26), as were Perez and Zerah (Gen. 38:1–30). In Genesis 5 from Seth to Noah the Scripture gives us the age of each patriarch when his wife bore their first son. Noah was five hundred when he had Shem, Ham, and Japheth (Gen. 5:32), obviously triplets. Shem was older than Ham, and Ham was older than Japheth, but they were all born to Noah's wife when Noah was five hundred years old. Terah's sons, Abram, Nahor, and Haran, may have been triplets (Gen. 11:27–28).

porcupines (concubines) (1 Kings 11:3). Family life could not have been too good for Solomon. There must have been a lot of unhappy women, frustrated wives (not enough sex), and neglected children.

The Scripture informs us that Solomon's wives, many from other religious backgrounds who were polytheists, turned Solomon's heart from monotheism, his God (1 Kings 11:1–13). Here is an example in a nutshell how monotheism turns to polytheism. Evidently Solomon had a problem. His bigamy was a result of his lust and his unlimited power as a rich potentate. It resulted in unfaithfulness to his God and the destruction of his kingdom. Solomon's problem was not intellectual; he was a man of exceeding wisdom (1 Kings 4:29–34). Solomon, however, couldn't sublimate his passions. Solomon turned from God because of his immorality: "He loved many foreign women" (1 Kings 11:1). Solomon's problem was one of control. He couldn't deal with his freedom. Because he could, he did (there was no restraint). His better judgment went by the wayside. Solomon's lust alienated him from God.

Adam is to be commended for his monogyny. In a discussion about marriage in Matthew 19:1–10, Jesus used Adam and Eve as an example of God's intention regarding the marital relationship. God established monogyny for family life. Adam was monogamous.

7

Husband

Adam had an intimate relationship with God. He also had a relationship with other creatures of the creation. But we read God said, "It is not good that man should be alone; I will make him a helper comparable to him" (Gen. 2:18). Adam's vertical relationship with God was vital, his number-one-priority relationship. God started the family, making Eve and presenting her to Adam. Adam became a husband. Eve, Adam's wife, became his cardinal horizontal relationship above all other humans or creatures.

The priority relationship for Adam, however, was with God. The same is intended for every human being. Adam was created before Eve, not making Adam more important but stressing that his relationship with God was quintessential. Since Eve, made from Adam, was brought to Adam, it became law "Therefore a man shall leave his father and mother and be joined to his wife, and they shall be one flesh" (Gen. 2:24).

A person born in a family is to be taught about God and to come into a relationship with God in his or her home. Then later that person leaves home and cleaves to his or her spouse. Sooner or later the husband or wife in a godly relationship departs to be with the Lord. This means one's physical relationship with one's spouse is temporal or limited to time on earth. But one's relationship, godly connection with the Lord is eternal, beginning, ideally, prior to the husband-and-wife marriage and going beyond it—forever.

Eve's relationship to Adam was not to take the place of God's relationship to Adam but to enrich Adam's life. Eve was created for Adam's happiness and the completion of God's purpose. Adam needed a companion comparable to him—that is one who was also made in the image of God. She was Eve. Eve, too, was to find in Adam happiness and fulfillment, achieving the purpose of God. She—that is a woman—was to have a special blessing in birthing God—God being born into the world as Jesus, a human. (See Matt. 1:18–23).

Genesis 2:18–25 is the Scripture that gives us the historic information that God instituted the family. The family was created to have a husband and a wife. God, a husband, and a wife compose a family. This was ordered by God and is the will of God.

Adam and Eve's family relationship was tripartite. Often when people are going to get married they are counseled as a dyad—two people. The dyad relationship is stressed. Adam's family was tripartite. That is Adam's family consisted of a covenant agreement with God, who put Adam and Eve in the garden to tend it. They each had a relationship with God. Second, Adam had a relationship with Eve and Eve had a relationship with Adam. It is beautifully pictured in Ecclesiastes 4:9–12.

> Two are better than one, Because they have a good reward for their labor. For if they fall, one will lift up his companion. But woe to him who is alone when he falls, For he has no one to help him up. Again, if two lie down together, they will keep warm; But how can one be warm alone? Though one may be overpowered by another, two can withstand him, And a threefold cord is not quickly broken.

God in the family is the first cord of a threefold cord that makes the family strong. Living in the garden, in God's stewardship, fulfilling His purpose in creation, and worshipping Him the family is as God intended it to be.

It must be emphasized that *Adam was a husband*—the first husband. In Genesis 3:6 (NIV) Eve, gave fruit to her "husband," Adam. Adam, the first man, was Eve's husband. In 1 Corinthians 7:2 God tells us each woman is to have her own husband (Greek *Aner*—adult male). The husband is to love his wife (Eph. 5:28).

The love a husband gives his wife is a special kind of love. The word *love* in Ephesians 5:28 used in the Koine Greek of the New Testament is *agapao*, a love modeled after God's perfect love, a love that originates from the indwelling presence of God's Spirit. Read 1 Corinthians 13:4–7 for divine insight about the agape love of God. It is the greatest piece of literature ever written on love.

The husband is the family leader of the household. We see such leadership modeled with Joshua, the leader of Israel who replaced Moses. Joshua spoke to the Hebrew people, inspirationally declaring, "As for me and my household, we will serve the Lord" (Josh. 24:15 NIV).

Going further, the husband is a Christ figure (Eph. 5:17–33). Husbands are exhorted to love their wives as Christ loved the church and gave Himself for it. God did not model His idea for Christ and the church after Adam and Eve. God created Adam and Eve to prophetically foretell what He planned for His people as the bride of Christ and what would be accomplished through Christ as the Bridegroom of those who would be in a covenant relationship with Him, forever.

8

Wife—Eve

Adam had a wife, Eve, the first wife, and she was a literal person in history. By now you are probably thinking, we *are learning a great deal about Adam*. Some consider him a myth and by choice know little about him. But there is an abundance of information about Adam. He did have a wife and called her Eve. "Eve" means the mother of all living. Like Adam, the father of all who live on planet earth, Eve is the mother of all human beings on planet earth. It was Adam who named Eve: "And Adam called his wife's name Eve, because she was the mother of all living" (Gen. 3:20).

It was Adam and Eve—not Adam and Steve. If it had been Adam and Steve, we would not be here. In fact, because it later became Adam and Steve, or Eve and Eve, is part of the second reason why mythologies were invented resulting in polytheism. People wanted God out of His universe so they could do as they wanted immorally, men having sex with men and women having sex with women. Our resource, the Bible, teaches that God turned those lusting after such aberrations, perversions, over to a (reprobate mind KJV) depraved minds, to do what ought not to be done. (See Rom. 1:18–28 NIV).

From our resource on Adam, we know specifically that he was created first. There was no Eve. In Genesis 1 it's recorded that God created man in His own image, male and female (v. 27). In a summary of Adam's and Eve's creation (Gen. 2:7, 15–25), we are given more detail. God caused a deep sleep to fall on Adam, and out of his side God created woman— Eve. It should be noted that woman was taken from Adam's side, not his head to be over him or his feet to be under him, but from his side to be beside him. Woman is man's helper (Gen. 2:20). Adam and Eve side by side were to manage Eden.

It is translated that Eve was made from Adam's rib (Gen. 2:21–23). Did Adam have one less rib? Did Eve, after they started having children, and later when there were others and Adam had gone off on a business trip, have to count his ribs when he came home? Dr. Toyozo Nakarai taught on this passage in Genesis that the Hebrew word translated "rib" is a very difficult word to understand. I remember him saying, "We really don't know what it means." But what we do know, all mystery aside, is that Eve was made from the side of Adam.

Martin Luther liked to emphasize that the Hebrew word for "made" in Genesis 2:22, where God created Eve out of Adam, is "built." In other words, God built the woman, Eve, out of man, Adam. Luther notes, "Here Moses uses a new and unheard of expression, not the verb 'form' or 'create' but 'built.'" He says, "Others look for an allegory and say that the woman is called a building because of the analogy to the church."[26]

God built the woman out of Adam as Christ, the Second Adam, is building the church, His bride, out of His sacrifice He made for her on the cross. Remember Jesus on the cross had a spear thrust into His side (John 19:31–35). Out of His side came blood and water, something that physically happens when there is a ruptured heart. Someone has asked, "God, how much do you love me?" Jesus answered on the cross. He spread out His arms and died. Jesus died of a broken heart, having been rejected by the people of planet earth (John 1:10–11). His death was to

---

26 Jaroslav Pelikan, editor, *Luther's Works*, Volume 1, Genesis, (St. Louis, MO: Concordia Publishing House, 1950), 131.

purchase His bride. This is the message we see presaged in the building of Eve from Adam's side in Genesis 2:21–25. Adam's oracular relationship to Eve and the bearing of children illustrated God's intention to build a special people from planet earth for Himself, a new creation to inhabit His celestial realm, heaven itself.

Eve was Adam's helper, comparable to him (Gen. 2:20). It is not without significance that Jesus, who was God on earth as a human being, limiting Himself in the flesh to one place, referring to what was to take place after His resurrection from the dead, said He had to go away. But He taught that He would not leave us without a Helper. The word for Helper in the New King James Version of the Bible is translated from the Greek word *paraclete*. Paraclete literally means one who stands beside. The Paraclete or Helper is the Holy Spirit. The one who stood beside Adam, man, in Genesis was Eve. Eve foreshadowed the Paraclete.

In the same way Adam was a Christ figure, Eve is a Holy Spirit figure. It is the Holy Spirit who births people in Jesus Christ to be the bride of Christ through regeneration. The Holy Spirit alone gives *zoe*, the Greek word meaning new "life."[27] Zoe is life that comes out of a new birth. Humans have bios, life that emanates from their physical birth. Zoe is spiritual life that is generated from a second birth. The mother of all living, Eve, represents in Genesis, prophetically, God's purpose to build Himself a family of new beings in His image. Eve metaphorically is the paraclete, one who stands beside, the Holy Spirit, helper.

---

27 Gerhard Kittel, editor, *Theological Dictionary of the New Testament*, Volume II. (Stuttgart, Germany: W. Kohlmanner Verlag, 1991), 865.

9

One Flesh

Why contemplate "one flesh" when learning about Adam? Because when God made Eve out of Adam and presented Eve to Adam, it is astounding, but we know what Adam said. Adam said, "This is now bone of my bones and flesh of my flesh. She shall be called Woman, because she was taken out of man" (Gen. 2:23).

The very next verse in our resource begins with the word *therefore*. Therefore is there for a reason. It means what is about to be written is the result of the truth immediately preceding it. The reason "a man shall leave his father and mother and be joined to his wife and they become one flesh" is because Eve was bone of Adam's bones and flesh of Adam's flesh. Added to this divine arrangement is the fact that Adam and Eve "were both naked, the man and his wife, and they were not ashamed."

The word flesh in Hebrew is *basar*, and it literally means "flesh." It is the body or flesh of a person. In the New Testament the equivalent Greek word for flesh is *sarx*. Eve, being made of Adam, was literally of Adam, flesh of his flesh and bone of his bones. Eve was of Adam's *basar* or of Adam's *sarx*.

God therefore has declared when a man leaves his father and mother and marries a woman, they are to be considered one flesh. The woman, of course, also leaves her parents and is one flesh with her husband.

What's true for Adam and Eve can never be true for Adam and Steve or Eve and Eve. Adam and Eve, the father and mother of a child, birth a baby that is uniquely from their own flesh and their own bones. Adam and Steve and Eve and Eve cannot birth a baby, nor can they be one flesh.

One flesh further means coitus is for the male (husband) and the female (wife) in marriage. Following the wedding ceremony, it was traditionally understood that coition brought about the state of being one flesh. In some circumstances there was no ceremony and only a commitment followed by coitus. Sexual intercourse doesn't mean a man and woman are married, but one flesh refers to the act of sex in marriage. Tim and Beverly LaHaye, Christian counselors, call sexual intercourse "the act of marriage." In their book, *The Act of Marriage*, they write, "The act of marriage is that beautiful and intimate relationship shaped uniquely by a husband and wife in the privacy of their love—and it is sacred. In a real sense, God designed them for that relationship."[28]

Building on these foundational truths, digging deeper, one flesh indicates intimacy. Such intimacy based on the intent of God in marriage involves two people living together in a commitment that has to do with giving and receiving love. David and Jan Stoop in *The Intimacy Factor* indicate intimacy is "the joyful union that comes when two people learn together how to give love and how to accept love."[29] This is where love is consummated in sexual intercourse and sexual intercourse continues in a loving relationship. However, it important to know that intimacy is more than a sexual relationship. The Adams were naked and not ashamed, a subject to be scrutinized in chapter 10.

Another important aspect of one flesh is that the primary human relationship for a husband is with his wife and for a wife is with her husband. There are some counselors, like a popular radio commentator,

---

28 Tim and Beverly LaHaye, *The Act of Marriage*. (Grand Rapids, MI: Zondervan Publishing House, 1976), 37.

29 David and Jan Stoop, *The Intimacy Factor*. (Nashville, TN: Thomas Nelson Publishers, 1993), 41.

who stress that a mother's primary relationship is with her children. Adam and Eve illustrate primary relationship is vertical—the one we have with God. The primary human relationship is with one's spouse.

Genesis 2:24 is true of Adam and Eve and understood by them. It states, "Therefore a man shall leave his father and mother and be joined to his wife, and they shall become one flesh." When a person "leaves" home the primary human relationship is not with a parent but with one's spouse. I explain this with some detail in my book *A Paradigm for Marital Intimacy.*[30] Suffice it to note that normally a child grows into an adult and leaves his or her parents. The husband and wife remain. This time in married life has been referred to as that of the empty nest.

Husbands and wives know their children are their own flesh. In most instances, they hang in there with their children, sticking with them through thick and thin. As my father used to say, "Blood is thick." We have a profound loyalty to our children. Often married couples do not think the same way about their own relationship. Most would never think of divorcing a child, yet some divorce one another without much thought. Understand God has declared that a husband and a wife are one flesh. Adam and Eve were one flesh. All married couples are proclaimed by God to be one flesh.

The *teleos*, purpose of God, through one flesh, with a husband and a wife was to prefigure Christ's relationship with the people He is procuring for Himself in the celestial realm throughout eternity. Adam represents Christ and Eve the Holy Spirit or those filled with the Spirit, the people who are the bride of Christ. Consider the following taught by the apostle Paul in Ephesians 5:30–33:

1. The Christian's relationship with Christ is likened to that Eve had with Adam. In Ephesians 5:30, of Jesus

---

30   Richard C. Besteder, *A Paradigm For Marital Intimacy at Westshore Christian Church.* (Ann Arbor, MI: UMI Dissertation Services, 1996), 40, 94–111.

Christ, Paul writes, "For we are members of His body, of His flesh and of His bones."

2. The reason God instituted the family with marriage between a man and a woman, a husband and a wife, in the context of Ephesians 5:30, is given in Ephesians 5:31: "For this reason a man shall leave his father and mother and be joined to his wife, and the two shall be one flesh."

3. Our resource on this subject, Scripture, tells us marriage is to teach us about Christ and the Church. Ephesians 5:32 says, "This is a great mystery, but I speak concerning Christ and the Church."

4. The result of Adam and Eve, of marriage, and God's purpose, right now, is for a husband and wife to live in an intimate and fulfilling relationship with one another, giving glory to God—Ephesians 5:33 "Nevertheless let each one of you in particular so love his own wife as himself, and let the wife see that she respects her husband."

Understanding God's beautiful plan for humankind gives us positive input why divorce is not the will of God. (See Matthew 19:1–10.) Jesus Christ would never divorce His bride. Nothing can separate His people from His love (Rom. 8:31–39). Those who are one flesh with Christ Jesus—the Bridegroom—know they are forever secure. Marriage is to teach us that lesson. See *A Paradigm for Marital Intimacy* for more perspective on the topic of the Bridegroom and the church as they relate to marriage.[31] From the beginning God instructs us on these truths through Adam and Eve. God purposely arranged and determined Adam and Eve's relationship so the two were one flesh.

---

31   Ibid., 33–43.

Before leaving the subject of one flesh, it is significant to note that the child of a husband and wife renders additional understanding on one flesh. Every person born on planet earth is mystically a unique person, a living soul, made in the image of his or her father and mother. Such is only possible through the one-flesh arrangement in the God-instituted family of Adam and Eve. What God does in the one-flesh creative sexual relationship of a husband and wife is beautiful beyond description. There is no acceptable way to change it or to improve upon it. It is the work of God!

Adam and Eve

Adam lay with ecstatic visions of something beautiful dancing colorfully in his head. The light of Elohim—purples, violets, blues, greens, yellows, oranges, and reds—kaleidoscopically formed endless variegated images in his mind. Though semiconscious, Adam's face sparkled with anticipatory delight. Adam smiled and smiled. The smiles were only interrupted by interspersed laughter and continuous intermittent moans of a spirit soothing and caressing.

Had not the Creator said, "Today is the day, oh Adam. Rejoice and be glad in it, for today I will make a woman, your helpmate. Woman shall come from you side, and she will be bone of your bones and flesh of your flesh. You are to love her as your own flesh, for indeed she will be of your flesh." The Creator told Adam to lie down. Adam remembered lying down. And now it was happening.

Adam thought, *What is love? How do I do it? The Creator is so good. Everything He does is good. Everything He makes is good. This thing called love must be good. What is my God teaching me? Where is all this going?*

It seemed but a moment, Adam's eyes opened slowly and adjusted. He sat up. He felt fine. He looked over his body. As far as he could see and feel, all was the same as before; or was it!

Then Adam heard the voice of God: "Adam." Adam stood and looked. There she was. Adam's mouth hung open, his eyes seemed to enlarge, and his head began to spin. Adam said, "Wow!" Adam repeated, "Wow!" Adam exclaimed, "Wow—wow—wow!" For a while, all Adam could say was, "*Wow!*"

10

Naked and Not Ashamed

Adam and Eve "were both naked, and they felt no shame" (Gen. 2:25 NIV). Adam and Eve in the garden, as husband and wife, were not clothed. Do not equate their nakedness with primitiveness. All things considered, Adam and Eve were more sophisticated than anyone in contemporary society. They were made by an extraterrestrial intelligence One beyond our ability to comprehend (more about this in another chapter). Adam and Eve were created on planet earth far superior to present-day humans in intelligence, stature, and longevity.

The Hebrew word for nakedness in Genesis 2:25 is *arom*.[32] Dietrich Bonhoeffer, a German scholar of the World War II era, saw this nakedness as innocence. He saw it as "the essence of unity and unbrokenness, of being for the other, of objectivity, of the recognition of the other in his right, in his limiting me and in his creatureliness."[33] Adam was literally naked before God and before Eve, his wife. The same was true for Eve. She was naked before God and Adam. Their nakedness, corporately and individually, had to do with more than naked bodies. Adam's *arom*

---

32 John H. Sailhammer, *The Expositor's Bible Commentary*, Volume 2, Genesis. (Grand Rapids, MI: Zondervan Publishing House, 1981), 49.

33 Dietrich Bonhoeffer, *Creation and Fall.* (New York: MacMilian Publishing Company, 1937), 78–79.

was a perfect transparency and honesty. There were no lies, no deceit, no hidden motives, and no malice. Summing it up, nothing was amiss. All was well—good in Eden.

The French philosopher Jean-Jacques Rousseau's writings, foreshadowing Romanticism, recognized a return to a natural idyll setting brings out the best in people.[34] The American writer Henry David Thoreau advocated a number of significant ideas, among them, living in harmony with nature. He wrote, "The mass of men lead lives of quiet desperation." *"He appealed to people to economize, to simplify their lives, and thus to save the time and energy that will allow them to live deep and suck out the marrow of life."*[35] These are worthy ideas. Hence many people came to romanticize the noble Native Americans, often in a semi-naked state. Adam and Eve however lived in an entirely different world. The nakedness of Romanticism is different than that of Adam and Eve.

In Genesis 3:7 Adam and Eve, having disobeyed God, found themselves naked and ashamed. The Hebrew word for nakedness there is different than that used in Genesis 2:25. Adam and Eve's nakedness, *arom*, noted in Genesis 2:25, instructs us about the wonderful innocence and purity of Adam and Eve, their intimate relationship with God in that innocence and with each other. The word for nakedness in Genesis 3:7, after Adam and Eve sinned, is *erom*.[36] *Erom* studied in context, like in Deuteronomy 28:48, where the Israelites are depicted in a condition brought about by their lack of trust in God, has to do with a nakedness that is directly opposite of *arom*. It is a nakedness of shame. Nakedness itself as either good or bad depends upon context. Know, then, that the meaning of nakedness for Adam and Eve, after their fall, changed.

---

34   Jean Terrasse, *World Book*, Volume 16. (Chicago: A Scott Fetzer Company, 2003), 492–3.

35   John Clendenning, *World Book*, Volume 19. (Chicago: A Scott Fetzer Company, 2003), 265–6.

36   John H. Sailhammer, *The Expositor's Bible Commentary*, Volume 2, Genesis. (Grand Rapids, MI: Zondervan Publishing House, 1983), 49.

Going further, nakedness in the husband and wife relationship heralds the uniqueness of a God-approved arrangement. Some nakedness today, however, belies shame. It is not appropriate for a husband and wife to get naked in front of others. A husband and wife's nakedness is reserved for each other—one's spouse. Leviticus 18 gives God directed specifics prohibiting various situations of nakedness, ones that are *erom*, not *arom*.

The exclusiveness of Adam and Eve's nakedness distinguishes the significance of a husband-and-wife relationship with each other as over and against their relationship with their children. A mother or dad does not get naked for the purpose of sex with one of his or her children. In nakedness we see God's purpose intentionally and practically in differentiating the relationship of a husband and wife from that of the children. Husbands and wives are to include nakedness in prioritizing the bonds they have with each other.

Children are not part of the nakedness arrangement, especially since the fall has changed its context. They are to be loved and nurtured in individualization and maturation, preparing them for the time when they will leave and establish their own homes. The best environment a father and mother can provide children in the home for intellectual, spiritual, and psychological health is to love one another. In our resource, the primary relationship God singles out for nakedness is for a husband and a wife. A man's nakedness is for his wife, and a wife's nakedness is for her husband. Such nakedness does not extend to children and others.

The nakedness of Adam and Eve signifies comfort with their surroundings in creation. They were in harmony with their Creator and with each other. Each one was in harmony with self, congruent. Adam and Eve were mentally and spiritually healthy—wholesome. That's what our resource means about Adam and Eve when it records they were naked and not ashamed.

11

Marriage

Adam was married. "Then the Lord made a woman from the rib (part) he had taken out of the man, and he brought her to the man" (Gen. 2:22 NIV). God brought the woman Eve to the man Adam. The relationship of a man and a woman, a husband and a wife, in marriage is sacred (set aside as special by God).

It's a gargantuan insight to know there were not eons and eons of animal life until one day two creatures, a male and female, became sophisticated enough to live together in an arrangement that could be called marriage. It takes a Herculean effort to envision, in all its aspects, how that could possibly have happened. In Genesis 2:22, it is simple; God established marriage.

Marriage has to do with male and female humans created in the image of God becoming one flesh, being naked and not ashamed in a relationship ordained and blessed by God. All points already expounded on Adam have been developed from the Scripture, not psychology, the study of human behavior. Psychology is a worthy endeavor that can bless human relationships. In the Scripture, however, we have God's intended principles through which the Living God works to bless and make happy, enriched, and successful the marriage of a husband and wife.

As already noted, love should be in the marriage relationship. From the beginning God loved the world (John 3:16). God's benevolent hand is seen everywhere in His providence and plan for mankind in Jesus Christ. Love is an attribute of God. God is Love (1 John 4:16). A happy marriage will have *agape* love (Holy Spirit love), *philia* love (the highest kind of human love), and *eros* love (love expressed in the sex act between a husband and wife).[37]

Assuredly, love was in the marriage of Adam and Eve. If you're working out of a God-directed, non-evolutionary perspective, love, like a great number of other particulars, is another factor of major importance among humans that is inexplicable. Creation accounts for a man being highly intelligent, like God, a being of love. The character of God, love, part of His image, permeated the relationship of Adam and Eve. It was so in marriage from the beginning.

Understand that although marriage is approved by God, it is not His will for everyone. You don't have to get married to please God. The Son of God, Jesus, was not married. The Scripture teaches Jesus was without sin in Hebrews 4:14–15.

> Seeing we have a Great High Priest who has passed through the Heavens, Jesus the Son of God, let us hold fast our confession. For we do not have a High Priest who cannot sympathize with our weakness, but was in all points tempted as we are, yet without sin.

(There are numerous other verses that teach the same truth. By the way, how many times does something have to be recorded in Scripture to be true? The answer is one. If something is true one time, it's true.) Jesus was perfect, the most whole and complete human being who ever lived on earth. And He was not married. Jesus also taught,

---

37   Richard C. Besteder, *A Paradigm For Marital Intimacy At Westshore Christian Church*. (Ann Arbor, MI: UMI Dissertation Services, 1996), 199–200.

There are eunuchs who were born thus from their mother's womb, and there are eunuchs who were made eunuchs by men, and there are eunuchs who have made themselves eunuchs for the kingdom of heaven's sake. (Matt. 19:12)

A eunuch was a castrated man. Jesus taught some men were castrated by others who used them as servants or slaves like to manage their harem. He said some were born as eunuchs, meaning they had no sexual proclivities and thus would not marry. Others Jesus said, though not castrated, would chose to serve God in a kind of ministry, building the kingdom of God, living the kind of servant life that would preclude them from marrying.

The life and teachings of Jesus negate the idea that a person is incomplete unless married. Some have speculated Adam was incomplete and God made Eve to complete him. The idea is that masculine is positive and feminine is negative. It's hypothesized that without a married partner of the opposite sex, a person is not balanced. If that's true, Jesus was incomplete, or any person not married is not a whole person. Such is simply not true. Adam was a perfect man. He didn't need Eve to complete him. Furthermore, to teach a person not married is an incomplete person is an insult to people who are single or who chose not to marry.

Referencing Genesis 2:18, Martin Luther believed that God was not referring to marriage. He wrote, "When God says not good that a man should be alone, of what good could he be speaking, since Adam was righteous and had no need of a woman as we have." Luther thought God was speaking of the common good and not personal good. He used "good" in this passage to denote the increase of the human race. Luther then saw Eve as necessary to carry out God's plan, with Adam to secure increase.[38]

---

38 Jaroslav Pelikan, *Luther's Works*, Volume I, Genesis. (St. Louis, MO: Concordia Publishing House, 1958), 115.

It is true that a loving husband can teach a woman many helpful things about a healthy masculinity. A loving wife can teach a husband helpful things about a healthy femininity. Each can be and should be good for each other. Marriage is a God-arranged, empirical relationship to bring individuals to spiritual maturity in loving God and psychological wholeness in humanly loving one's spouse.

But the person who relies on another human to meet his or her need is building a dysfunctional relationship and developing a troubled personhood. Only God, Christ, is adequate to meet our need fully.[39] When one tries to change the other person to be what that one wants him or her to be and when one expects his or her spouse to make one feel adequate or significant, one is going to become critical, angry, and unsatisfied with the relationship.[40] Adam was complete before Eve arrived because God satisfied his innermost need. God completed Adam.

Do not get married to be whole through another person. The logical scheme of things in Genesis is God first and a spouse second. A group called the Navigators has the right approach on this one. They teach one should get right with God first, get healthy, and then get married. Be spiritually healthy and well so you can bless your spouse. To be blessed, or to be well, marry someone who has spiritual wellness and strength from the Lord. Marriage doesn't make people well. God blesses well people in marriage and makes them better.

While many people today place most emphasis on a wedding ceremony, it is more important for a couple to have a good relationship. The Scripture gives divine insight on relationship in marriage that prompts us to prioritize it. In Deuteronomy 24:5 instructions are given to a newly married man. "He shall not go out to war or be charged with any business; he shall be free at home one year, and bring happiness to his

---

39   Lawrence J. Crabb Jr., *The Marriage Builder.* (Grand Rapids, MI: Pyranee Books, 1982), 71–72.

40   Ibid., 20–21.

wife whom he has taken." God's Word calls for a time of adjustment at the outset of marriage to build the husband and wife relationship. In psychology we call such special time "bonding."[41]

In marriage we do not complete one another, but we do complement one another. There are needs a person has that God wills the spouse to fulfill.[42] Being there for the other is one. Marriage involves a lifetime commitment. Adam, we always remember, was the man for Eve. Eve, we always remember, was the woman for Adam. When we think of marriage, we think of Adam and Eve. One's marriage should be prioritized. Your marriage is more important than your bank account, your entertainment, or your vocation.[43]

As a chaplain in the US Air Force I've seen marriages that were failing turn around and blossom when married couples made marriage their number-one commitment and in love gave up priorities that were destroying their relationship. Without commitment, there is not really a marriage or workable love. There is no security or trust.

---

41 Richard C. Besteder, *A Paradigm for Marital Intimacy at Westshore Christian Church*. (Ann Arbor, MI: UMI Dissertation Services, 1996), 113–38.

42 Lawrence J. Crabb Jr., *The Marriage Builder*. (Grand Rapids, MI, Pyranee Books, 1982), 70–71.

43 Richard C. Besteder, *A Paradigm for Marital Intimacy at Westshore Christian Church*. (Ann Arbor, MI: UMI Dissertation Services, 1996), 24.

12

Gardeners

The Adam's were gardeners by vocation. When I was a chaplain in the US Air Force, often a person I met would ask, "What kind of a chaplain are you?" My answer was, "A good one." What kind of gardener was Adam? The answer is a good one!

God said to Adam and Eve,

> Be fruitful and multiply; fill the earth and subdue it, have dominion over the fish of the sea, over the birds of the air, and over every living thing that moves on the earth … See, I have given you every herb that yields seed which is on the face of all the earth, and every tree whose fruit yields seed; to you it shall be for food. Also, to every beast of the earth, to every bird of the air, and to everything that creeps on the earth, in which there is life, I have given every green herb for food; and it was so. (Gen. 1:28–30)

Adam and Eve were coworkers in Eden, God's garden. God put them in charge of the earth (Gen. 1:28), twenty-five thousand miles in circumference the greatest real estate project in the history of our planet. Adam and Eve had dominion over creatures, trees, and plants—over everything. They were to have children and populate the earth. Adam and Eve belonged to God. The earth belonged to God. All the people of the planet were to serve God. We learn from the instructions and enlightenment of our resource that all of us are made in the image of God and that we exist for God's purpose in the celestial realm (1 Cor. 15:47–49).

Adam named all the cattle, the birds of the air, and every beast of the field (Gen. 2:19–20). He also named Eve (Gen. 3:20). Certainly Adam named plants and trees, classifying them as we do. Adam spent time with Eve, bonding with her, as God later taught the Israelites to do (Deut. 24:5). Adam took the information God gave him and philosophized (Gen. 2:23).

All the constructive things we do today are a continuation of what God began in Adam. What we call science is simply discovering what God gave us in creation and putting it to practical use. Whether we are studying the eye and how it works, waves in the air for operating our radios and televisions, or whatever, we marvel at the Master Intelligence who devised it all. We note intelligent design like in the complexity of the cell, specifically the DNA and how it works.[44]

It is significant that God put Adam on planet earth and gave him responsibly for it. We don't know how much of the planet was like Eden, and we might assume, before the fall, Adam could exit Eden and return. We don't know if animals died prior to Adam and Eve's disobedience (we'll look at this perspective under the "Tree of Life") or whether they died on other parts of the earth but not in Eden. There are many questions we could ask for which we have no answers.

I once made an arrangement with an airman to teach a Bible class. He returned after the first session greatly flustered. "The class," he blurted

---

44   Lee Strobel, *The Case For A Creator.* (Grand Rapids, MI: Zondervan, 2004), 193–246.

out, "asked me many questions that I could not answer." I quoted to him Deuteronomy 29:29: "The secret things belong to the Lord our God, but those things which are revealed belong to us and our children forever that we may do all the works of the law." I told him, "We are not under the Law but under the gospel of grace. The principle, however, is the same. We don't have to explain everything because God has not revealed everything to us. What God has revealed is sufficient. We do know a great deal from what has been revealed!"

We don't know where Eden was located. Some suggest it was in the area of present-day Kuwait. Others think it was little further south, now underwater in the northern part of the Persian Gulf. My wife is sure it was in Florida.

We don't know how old our planet is. The Scripture doesn't tell us, probably because we don't need to know. The Hebrew word for day is *yom*, which can mean a twenty-four-hour period or an indefinite period of time. If you believe the earth was created in six twenty-four-hour days, that still doesn't tell you how old our planet is. Bishop Usher, coordinating dates in history with biblical people, used genealogical dates counting back to Adam to conclude the earth was about six thousand years old. However, we do not know how long Adam and Eve, having access to the Tree of Life, were in the garden before they were expelled because of their disobedience (more about this later).[45] Conflict occurs between people of varying viewpoints when some are adamant about matters not explicitly revealed in our resource, the Scripture.

It would be anachronistic to think Adam and Eve were involved in ecology. In the beginning God had every part of His Creation in perfect balance. It's humankind that has polluted our streams and air, committing horrendous atrocities. As an example, certain elements of our culture here in the United States, motivated by greed, killed off most of the buffalo, beaver, and white-tailed deer. I have confidence that

---

45 See chapter 44 on longevity.

if Adam could be with us today, it would not take him long to get up to speed on ecology. Adam would not be pleased. As descendants of Adam, we are responsible, under God's supervision, to take care of the earth.

Our greatest task in knowing about Adam is trying to earnestly understand the input we are given about him in our resource. One must think big. We begin with God—"In the beginning God created the heavens and the earth" (Gen. 1:1 NIV). The God presented in our resource, the Bible, is totally awesome. The first man, Adam, gives us the big picture. Everything in God's plan for human history begins with Adam. The first man, Adam, was a gardener, the gardener. Everything began in a garden.

Some historians' teaching on our past claim civilization began in cities. Actually, until the Industrial Revolution, beginning in England during the 1700s, most of earth's human population lived in rural settings.[46] Thomas Jefferson, the third president of the United States, said, "I view great cities as pestilential to the morals and the liberties of Man."[47] Jefferson, some of Adam's character shining in him, busied himself inventing things, classifying plants and animals, working a few small businesses, creating a unique garden with rare specimens, and primarily farming, which was his main means of support.[48]

It is amusing too that Diocletian, one of Rome's emperors, in his later life found gardening more rewarding than being the emperor of Rome, the world's greatest empire. Diocletian divided the Roman Empire into the east and west. He appointed Maximian as emperor in the west. They ruled as co-emperors, with a Caesar under each of them. Maximian had agreed to resign if Diocletian ever decided to do so. Diocletian was the first emperor to resign. When he resigned, he retired to a remote

---

46 Jean Cooke, Ann Kramer, Theodore Rowland-Entwistle, *History's Timeline*. (New York: Barnes and Noble, 1996), 162.

47 Carter Smith, *Presidents—All You Need To Know*. (Irving, NY: Hylas Publishing, 2005), 28.

48 Saul K. Padover, *Jefferson*. (New York: Penguin Group, 1952), 161–2.

area where he spent his time "in building, planting, and gardening."[49] Edward Gibbon writes in *The Decline and Fall of The Roman Empire* that Maximian solicited Diocletian to reassume the reign of government, the imperial purple. Diocletian:

> Rejected the temptation with a smile of pity, calmly observing that, if he could show Maximian the cabbages which he had planted with his own hands at Salona, he should no longer be urged to relinquish the enjoyment of happiness for the pursuit of power."[50]

Gardening is choice.

If aliens made a planet and put life on it, what would it be like? Would you imagine edifices, some kind of domes made of glass, computers galore, shiny objects that streak through the sky, saucers descending from the heavens and others ascending, weapons that could vaporize enemies, and sophisticated robots everywhere?

Some among us could conjure up detailed, amazing theoretical entities with all sorts of fantastic designs and mind-boggling technical equipment. We could visualize such a world because we are made in the image of God—that is, we are beings capable of fanciful creativity. The creature world cannot do such things.

What did God do? He made a world with a perfect, amazing, man in a beautiful garden, a veritable paradise. Eden means "enchantment" or "pleasure." The garden contained all sorts of created living things, plants, trees, and creatures—birds, fish, and animals, including Adam and Eve, all of it wonderful, almost beyond description in composition and operation. God made a setting that mankind could not visualize or duplicate—the

---

49   Edward Gibeon, *The Decline and Fall of the Roman Empire*, Great Books. (Chicago: Encyclopaedia Britannica, Inc., 1988), 157.

50   Ibid.

man and woman in the garden, interrelating with Him, each other, and the life surrounding them, in purpose and perpetual joy.

As Job, in the early history of mankind observed, "man was placed on the earth" (Job 20:4 NIV). Mankind did not come out of the earth but was placed on the earth by a Creative Intelligence. You can think of God as alien life, alien in that He is transcendent and has His throne above, in a place called heaven. God, however, is not an alien because He made the world, and it is His world, a world in which He is present, working His will through His chosen vessels.

Yes, "O Lord [our Creator], our Lord, how majestic is your name in all the earth!" (Ps. 8:9 NIV)

13

Spirit

Adam was a spirit in a body. Every person on planet earth is a spirit in a body. The spirit of a man cannot be seen through a microscope. Mankind cannot devise an instrument to measure the spirit of another human. Mankind cannot create a spirit. Only God can create a spirit. Only God can create a man. Only God could create Adam. God created Adam as a spirit in a body!

God made Adam out of the elements of the earth. Adam had a physical body, but Adam became a man when God breathed into him the breath of life (Gen. 2:7). God is Spirit (John 4:24). Spirit is like the wind (see John 3:6–8). When God breathed into Adam and put *ruah*, spirit, in Adam, Adam became a living soul.

The soul is a spirit in a body. It is not a physical part of a person's anatomy. Taking our resource or record of creation serious, a soul is *nephesh*, the life of a human, one's entire personality.[51] Basically, a soul is both a person's spirit and body. The body is perceived outwardly, recognized physically, as an individual person. Going deeper, the soul is the actual inward life of a person. A person's spirit is only truly known by God.

---

51   Merrill F. Unger, *Unger's Bible Dictionary*. (Chicago: Moody Press, 1970), 1040.

Lee Strobel in *The Case for a Creator* writes about the reality of the soul. He indicates that a soul is different than one's consciousness. The soul is a person, the invisible person.[52] He's not writing about an individual's physical body. He's writing about what is called in 2 Corinthians 4:16 "the inward man": "Therefore we do not lose heart. Even though our outward man is perishing, yet the inward man is being renewed day by day." Augustine in his classic work, *The City of God*, wrote "While a man is alive, and body and soul are united, it [Scripture] calls each of them singly by the name 'man,' speaking of the soul as the 'inward man,' and of the body as the 'outward man.'"[53]

In the New Testament there is a reference to the body, spirit, and soul (1 Thess. 5:23). The spirit of a man needs to be redeemed because of sin. The new life that puts a person's spirit, soul, and body in fellowship with God is called *zoe* (John 1:12-13, 3:3-8, 10:10). A person without *zoe* has *bios*, which we know as biological life. Every person has bios and is a soul, life (spirit)—*psyche*.

The spirit of a person or life—*psyche*, soul—that is born again has *zoe*. That person is in a body, but the body tells us nothing about the spirit or type of life that person has with God. It is a person's spirit that tells us about that person. The only way we can take note of a person's spirit is by that person's behavior. We can modify our behavior to mislead others about who we really are, but God knows a person's heart—a person's spirit, the inner person (Matt. 15:19–20).

A man's spirit is eternal, immortal. Once created, the spirit lives forever. The body, however, is temporal. The body is spoken of as an earthly house or tent that is struck or destroyed (2 Cor. 5:1). So when a person's body is no longer functional, that body returns to the earth from whence it came.

---

52   Lee Strobel, *The Case For A Creator*, (Grand Rapids, Michigan, Zondervan, 2004), 259-261.

53   Augustine, translated by Rev. Marcus Dods, D.D., *The City of God, The Nicene and Post Nicene Fathers, Volume II St. Augustine.* (Grand Rapids, MI: Wm. B. Eerdmans Publishing Company, 1979), 259.

It goes to dust, and the spirit made by God returns to God. Writing on physical death, Solomon penned, "The dust will return to the earth as it was, And the spirit will return to God who gave it" (Eccl. 12:7).

Just because the spirit or soul (one's life, inner person) is eternal does not mean it will be with God in the afterlife.[54] God has a place for those who are to be with Him and a place set aside for those who are not to be with Him.

The view "the cosmos is all that there is" is blatantly false. To see everything from a materialistic viewpoint is to deny the existence of the spirit. To think all that is wondrously beautiful in mankind as simply a product of the intellect is astonishingly lacking in substance.[55] All that is inspirational and aesthetical in art, sculpture, architecture, music, drama, poetry, and literature in humankind originates out of the spirit.

Anyone who has ever competed in sports knows beyond one's skill, preparation, and strategy, winning, especially when an individual has a stellar performance, is a matter of spirit—one's spirit throughout the competition. The spirit in a person is what leads him or her to climb a mountain no one has climbed before or attempt a feat others think is impossible. Our indomitable spirit comes from God.

The fact that I am a spirit is another proof of my Creator that I am made in His image. The materialistic "survival of the fittest" philosophy

---

54 Ibid., 262. The essence of the soul is a person's spirit. Augustine wrote "for what is man's soul, if not spirit."

55 Federick C. Mish, editor in chief, *Merriam-Webster's Collegiate Dictionary, Tenth Edition.* (Springfield, MA: Merriam Webster, Incorporated, 1998), 717. Materialism is "a theory that physical matter is the only fundamental reality and that all being and processes and phenomena can be explained as manifestations or results of matter." The materialist assumes that intellect just evolved out of matter. The question not answered by the materialist is how the intellect, thinking, which is immaterial, developed out of the material. The Scripture sees humankind's ability to think rationally, the ability to make choices, as the result of being created in the image of God. This has to do with a person's spirit.

that sees a person as only a refined animal is awash in a sea of immoral ambivalence.[56] Such codswallop contributed immensely to a holocaust in places like Auschwitz and Treblinka.

Obviously one of the reasons for the great world religions, including Hinduism and Buddhism, has to do with humankind's spiritual nature—man's propensity to worship. It is an undeniable fact that the human race is spiritually inclined. For a person not to understand that we are spirits in bodies is like not being aware of the nose on your own face. It is in the world of the spirit that we begin to comprehend something of Adam and his world. It is in our spirits that we become aware of the mystery and overwhelming beauty of our world.

Adam, the perfect man, a spirit in a body, was in touch with his environment, spiritually sensitive, and finely tuned by His Creator with whom he had fellowship. We cannot begin to fathom the relationship Adam had with the animals in his world. One reason is because of our spiritual triviality in understanding life on our planet.

As with the buffalo, beaver, and white-tailed deer that were slaughtered literally by the hundreds of thousands, similarly we continue to see animal life existing only for our aggrandizement. We enjoy eating chickens, almost totally unaware of how brutally many chickens are bred and hastily prepared for our consumption. Who cares if these birds have no life and are horrendously abused and then slaughtered for our insatiable palatable sumptuousness? The same is true with beef. The point is, like our oceans are basically unexplored, we think we know

---

56 Augustine, translated by Rev. Marcus Dods, D.D., *The City of God, The Nicene And Post Nicene, Fathers, Volume II St. Augustine.* (Grand Rapids, MI: Wm B. Eerdmans Publishing Company, 1979), 260. Augustine in *The City of God* writes of mankind as animals with animated bodies in which the soul serves as the residence of sensation. He adds, "Man received a rational soul, which was not produced out of the waters and the earth like other living creatures, but was created by the breath of God. Yet this creature was so ordered that the human soul should live in an animal body, like those other animals of which the Scripture said, 'Let the earth produce every living soul,'" 260.

the animal world but we do not. Animals too are spirits with spirit sensitivity.[57]

It was through my daughter's parakeets that I came to understand that every bird, every animal, for that matter, has a peculiar personality and is unique in itself. God's creation is truly wonderful. Through my dog, Rot, I have come to understand an animal's individual personality, intelligence, and spiritual propensities. Most people reading this book will not have the slightest hint of what I'm writing about.

Some people like Steve Irwin have inspired us with their understanding and care for God's animal kingdom.[58] The other day there was a news clip on television of a woman's reunion with a lion she had rescued from a wilderness area. A considerable time had passed since she had given the lion to a zoo. It was inspiring, seeing the woman where she was not supposed to be, right up to the bars of the lion's enclosed area, and the great male lion with a majestic flowing mane reared up on its hind legs, front paws through the bars around the woman's neck, hugging the woman and affectionately licking her in the face.[59] Emotionally uplifting, the unusual scene was a brief glimpse of Adam in Eden and what is to come in Christ. Such is inspiring, thrilling!

---

57 Ibid., 243–4. Augustine knew that animals were souls. But it pleased God to create Adam, alone, in His image. Augustine believed in a literal Adam and Eve. The same God who created the universe or cosmos also created all the animals, souls as well as bodies. Among the terrestrial animals, man was made by Him, in His own image, and was made one individual, though he was not left solitary. See chapter three.

58 Steve Irwin was an Australian television personality and a world-famous wildlife expert and conservationist.

59 Although this lion greeted his deliverer and friend in an astoundingly mysterious and wondrous fashion, such interaction is the exception, not the rule. It teaches us there is more to animal and human relationships than is commonly recognized. Nevertheless, I counsel others not to so act with wild animals. For instance, be warned, a polar bear will eat you. Copying the woman seen on the evening television newsreel will probably mean your death.

Adam evidently communicated with animals. He was their friend, and they knew it. Like Jesus in the wilderness for forty days with wild beasts (Mark 1:12–13) and unhurt by them, so Adam understood the animals of his garden and they understood him. I have observed that my dog and other dogs seem able to sense the spirit of various human beings. I have also noticed that animals around where I have lived are able to sense one's spirit.

Job exhorted, "Ask the beasts and they will teach you: And the birds of the air, and they will tell you; or speak to the earth, and it will teach you: And the fish of the sea will explain to you" (Job 12:7–8). Job, of course, was talking about what God has done in His wisdom. Creation is full of spirits, animal life, made by God that can teach us about the spirit world. Get in touch, observe, and enjoy!

In summary, the immaterial cannot come from the material. The ethereal in Adam and the creation all around him points to the celestial. In the days of Adam, mankind had a different relationship with animals. The day will come again when a child will be able to play by the hole of the asp and all will be well (Isa. 11:1–9). Perhaps these are the days for which the Sioux did their Ghost Dance, the days when the buffalo will return. But know this—Adam was a spirit, a light to whom the animals of Eden were drawn. He knew them, and they knew him. How beautiful it is to be in the Spirit and to walk with God. Even the animals recognize it and are glad.

14

Creator

Adam was not. Then he was. Adam was created fully grown. He didn't have a mother or father. Adam, however, was a prototype for all that would follow. When Adam first came to consciousness, there was his Creator. Like the creation, Adam had a specific beginning in time and space.

"In the beginning God created the heavens and the earth" (Gen. 1:1). Our resource tells us there was a beginning—the Creator spoke. The Creator, by divine fiat, said, "Let there be light" (Gen. 1:3). Until that time, there was no matter. Scientists call this the big bang. It couldn't happen without a Creator. If a person is sitting on his front porch with a friend and he hears a loud bang, he would say something like, "Did you hear that loud noise? I wonder what caused it!" "I wonder what caused the big bang!" God caused the big bang! It's called creation.

There was nothing. God began time and space. The Creator, by His divine will, made our world ex nihilo—planet earth from nothing. God made things that are seen from things that are invisible (Heb. 11:3). God created Adam. Adam knew the Creator (Gen. 2:15—3:24). Adam passed on the knowledge of God as His Creator and about Him to future generations.

The Hebrew word for God in Genesis 1:1 is *Elohim*. A Hebrew word for God is *El*. Elohim is in the plural. Most Jewish interpreters indicate the plurality refers to the majesty of God. They have to so interpret because they do not believe in the Christian Godhead of Colossians 2:6–10. Some Christians interpret Elohim the same way because they believe Jewish folk are the experts about the Hebrew language of the Old Testament. But many Christians think Elohim refers to the Father, the Son, and the Holy Spirit. The Hebrew Scripture of the Bible clearly teaches the reality of the Godhead. In Isaiah 48:16–18 we read the words of Jesus, our Creator.

> Come near to Me, hear this: I have not spoken in secret from the beginning; From the time that it was, I was there. And now the Lord God and His Spirit have sent Me. Thus says the Lord Your Redeemer, The Holy One of Israel; I am your Lord your God, Who teaches you to profit, Who leads you by the way you should go. Oh, that you had heeded my commandments! Then your peace would have been like a river.

In the passage just quoted, the Holy One of Israel, the Lord, Israel's God, said He had been present from the beginning. It had not been a secret. He had communicated about the creation (from the beginning - to Adam) and since then (beginning with Adam) about God's plan. He was sent by the Lord God (the Father) and by His Spirit. Hence we have the Father, the (Holy) Spirit, and the one sent, the Son.

John the apostle wrote of Jesus,

> In the beginning was the Word, and the Word was with God, and the Word was God. He was in the beginning with God. All things were made through Him, and without Him nothing was made that was made … And the Word became flesh and dwelt among us, and we beheld His glory, the glory as of the only begotten of the Father, full of grace and truth" (John 1:1–3, 14)

Paul wrote about Jesus,

> He is the image of the invisible God, the firstborn over all creation. For by Him all things were created that are in heaven and that are on earth, visible and invisible, whether thrones or dominions or principalities or powers. All things were created through Him and for Him. And He is before all things, and in Him all things consist. (Col. 1:15–17)

I've heard commentators on television ask the question, "Are we alone on planet earth?" The answer is emphatically no! We are not alone. Angels, celestial beings, have visited our planet from its beginning. Some came to Abraham before Sodom and Gomorrah was destroyed (Gen. 18–19). Gabriel visited Mary in Luke 1:36–38. Two were at the tomb of Jesus on the morning of His resurrection (Luke 24:1–7).

Angels (the word angel means "messenger") are creations of God from another world. They don't arrive in spaceships. It's apish, sluggish in intelligence, to think there are aliens out there who have to arrive in some kind of spacecraft or use some sort of machines to function. The angels in our resource look just like we do. They come and go according to the purpose of their Creator.

In fact, the one true reality of our world is Christ Jesus. Our world has been visited by someone from outer space, and His name is Jesus. It's remarkable that there are those who claim everything that has happened in the development of the earth was by chance, all explainable by their view of science, yet they cannot explain how life began. Richard Dawkins, a nonbeliever in God or a Creator, in an interview with Ben Stein in *Expelled*[60] when pressed on this issue fell back to the thesis that maybe aliens started life. He is correct. Not aliens but *someone from above* did start life on earth. His name is Jesus. The Creator of Adam was the Son of God, the preexistent Jesus.

---

60   Ben Stein, *Expelled*. (Universal City, CA: Vivendi Entertainment, DVD).

The apostle John, in his gospel two thousand years ago, had a space theology in which he followed the theme that Jesus was from another World. John writes about Jesus being God who made all things and is Light—the light of mankind: "The true Light which gives light to every man coming into the world. He was in the world, and the world was made through Him, and the world did not know Him" (John 1:9–10).

Later in John's gospel, when Jesus was being verbally assaulted by the religious leaders of Jerusalem, Jesus talked about going away. He was referring to His ascension back to heaven after His death, burial, and resurrection (John 8:21–22). Jesus had told those attacking Him that they could not go to where He was going. No one can go where Jesus is unless God transports him or her there. The religious leaders were puzzled as to where He was going and why they could not follow. Then Jesus uttered these astounding words: *"You are from below; I am from above. You are of this world, I am not of this world"* (John 8:23 NIV).

John continued with this theme when Jesus was questioned by Pilate. Pilate held in his hands the power to keep Jesus from dying on the cross or to condemn Him. He was amazed and awed by Jesus. Pilate had never met anyone like Him. An intelligent man, skilled in interrogation, he suspected Jesus was not of this world. Jesus had told Pilate that His kingdom was not of this world. Pilate asked, "Where do you come from?" (John 19:9 NIV) That's right—Pilate guessed it. Jesus was not from this world.

If the intelligence that created the world wanted to visit our planet to work out His purpose, how would He come? Some folks are continually talking about unidentified objects in the sky—spacecraft—operated by some kind of secretive, bashful type of creatures who are always coming and going but never really make themselves known. Our Creator however made Himself known. The Creator did something only our Creator could do—something too wise for the apish to understand.

The Creator became a creature. He came born as a baby out of a woman named Mary. We read about it in Matthew 1:23 concerning the birth of Jesus—Emmanuel, God with us. It was foretold by the prophet Isaiah in Isaiah 7:14. It's called the incarnation—God becoming human flesh. It's wonderful beyond description. And that's why billions of people every year celebrate His birth in the most glorious day ever to grace planet earth—Christmas.

If Adam was among us and was a name dropper, he would be a continuous world celebrity. He personally knew the Creator. The fact that Jesus visited us is easily verified in history.[61] It isn't that it's studied and found wanting. It's that some people seek to explain life by digging for old bones they claim are millions of years old rather than learning about the living Creator who visited our planet less than two thousand years ago.

Some have a problem with Jesus walking on water, raising the dead, and causing the blind to see and the lame to walk. But wouldn't you expect the personage who was able to create our World by divine fiat would be able to do such things? Yes, He worked miracles. Isn't that the point? The miraculous indicates who He is!

Adam's Creator, our Creator, and our God, is alive and well. Millions know Him personally. He testifies of His reality every day by answered prayer. Not only did He create Adam but He has continued to create. He is still creating today. Some adhere to unbelief because they say we are on a small planet and insignificant beings. Such are the views of the apish. Those being molded, God's special creation, understand what is happening in them every day and that they are being fashioned to populate an eternal home in a new life beyond the blue. Adam had a Creator. You and I have a Creator too. His name is Jesus. Hallelujah!

---

61   Lee Strobel, a formal skeptic, an award-winning journalist, and a Christian author, wrote a number of excellent books that powerfully and convincingly present *The Case for a Creator*, *The Case for Faith*, *The Case for Christ*, and *The Case for the Real Jesus*.

15

The Aura

Adam was encapsulated in an ethereal light—an aura. *Halley's Bible Handbook*, on Genesis 2:25, Adam being naked without shame suggests of Adam and Eve, "It may be they were clothed with ethereal light, as Jesus was when he was transfigured (Mark 9:3)."[62]

> That light vanished when sin entered—but it will one day again cloth the Redeemed (Revelation 3:4; 21:23). Of all God's creatures, as far as we know, humanity along wears clothing, a badge of our sinful nature and a symbol of our need of Redemptive covering.[63]

Our resource, the Scripture, informs us that God is Light (1 John 1:5). Psalm 104:1 pictures God covered with light as with a garment. The Greek word for glory, *doxa* in the New Testament, has as its first meaning literally, light. One gets the idea of glory as light when we read about the angel who appeared to the shepherds to announce the birth of Jesus. Luke wrote about the shepherds in the presence of heavenly beings, angels, recording, "The glory of the Lord (bright light) shone around them" (Luke 2:9 NIV).

---

62 Henry Hampton Halley, *Halley's Bible Handbook*, (Grand Rapids, Michigan, Zondervan Publishing House, 2000), 91-92.

63 Ibid., 92.

God, the Creator, present with Adam, resulted in the glory of the Lord shining around Adam—as an aura. It would have been impossible for Adam to be with God and not have an aura of glory or radiant light emitting from his presence.

When Moses led the Israelites out of Egypt during their time in the wilderness, Moses alone with God asked, "Please show me your glory" (Ex. 33:18). God told Moses, "You cannot see my face; for no man shall see Me, and live" (Ex. 33:20). It is difficult to look at the sun at its brightest. If a person in the flesh could behold God, who made the sun, it would result in instant vaporization. Nevertheless, God put Moses in the cleft of a rock and passed by, letting Moses see a portion of His toned-down glory.

When Moses returned to the Israelites from conversing with God, he did not know that his face shone brightly. People were afraid of him. Trying to look at him was as difficult as trying to look at the sun in its glory. So Moses, when among the people, had to wear a veil. He would take the veil off when he went to talk with God and put it back on when he was going to be among the Israelites (Ex. 34:29–35). As time passed, eventually, the glory or light from Moses' face would fade (2 Cor. 3:7–18).

A Christian's inner person, spirit, is being transformed daily into the glory of the image of Jesus Christ, a glory that does not fade away. The Christian in this divine process will be transformed into a glorified being of the celestial realm to be present eternally with our Lord and King, Jesus (2 Cor. 3:18, 4:16, 5:1; 1 Cor. 15:47–49). This transformation, translated from the Greek word *metemorphoo*, is the same word we use in biology to describe what happens when a caterpillar becomes a butterfly. It's also the same word used in Matthew 17:1–9 to describe the transfiguration of Jesus (when Jesus was illuminated and shone like a bright light). Such is the ultimate purpose of the Creator—that is to create beings, sons and daughters of God, Adam's offspring, personages of glory (2 Cor. 5:17, Heb. 2:10).

In the beginning Adam and Eve reflected the glory of God. Their aura set them apart from the rest of God's creatures. All creatures knew when Adam and Eve were around. Adam and Eve were obviously held in awe by all of God's creatures. You might notice they were not identified by the color of their skin. The Bible places no emphasis on an individual's skin color. Adam and Eve were identified by light—their aura.

16

Lucifer

"Evil company corrupts good habits" (1 Cor. 15:33). Everything God made on planet earth in the creation was good (Gen. 1:4, 10, 12, 18, 21, 25, 31). There was one who came to the garden who was not good. In Isaiah 14:12 he is called Lucifer, which means "shining star."

Lucifer was present among Adam and Eve. Evidently Lucifer was once a good angelic being. He is called a morning star in Isaiah 14:12. In the book of Job he is called Satan (adversary) and is among the sons of God coming into the presence of God. For space theology he is called "the ruler of the kingdom of the air" in Ephesians 2:2 (NIV). Like other celestial beings that visit planet earth, Lucifer travels through space. He is a spirit, which means he is invisible. In Eden Lucifer entered into the body of a serpent. He spoke through the serpent to disrupt God's work with planet earth.

Our resource doesn't tell us whether Adam knew Lucifer was present. When Eve spoke to him, she might not have known to whom she was speaking. She thought she was speaking to the serpent. We are taught that Lucifer invented the lie. Jesus called him the Devil (Accuser) in John 8:44, a murderer and a liar, the father of both. Lucifer is a deceiver. He deceived Eve.

One cannot understand Adam and Eve, what happened in the garden, the Bible, or what happens in our world today unless one understands the reality of Lucifer. The Bible makes absolutely no sense if you eliminate the supernatural, namely God. Nor will it make any sense if one eliminates Lucifer, his work, and the work of the celestial powers he controls. The apostle Paul, teaching Christians on spiritual warfare, wrote, our struggle is not against flesh and blood, "but against the rulers, against the authorities, against the powers of this dark world, and against the spiritual forces of evil in the heavenly realms" (Eph. 6:12 NIV).

Lucifer was not part of God's work in the creation of planet earth. God created beings with a free will. He wants those who worship Him to do so because they love Him. Lucifer, wanting to be God (Isa. 14:12–14), led a revolt against God. One third of heaven was led astray (Rev. 12:7–9). Some speculate the reason God created planet earth was to populate heaven with replacements for those lost in Satan's rebellion. This may or may not be true. God, however, when all is examined, determines a high purpose for His people: that they go from planet earth to heavenly realms. The future of a person in Christ is to rule with Him in celestial glory. The Christian is a joint-heir with Christ (Rom. 8:17). The apostle Paul taught concerning Christians that all is ours (1 Cor. 3:21–23).

Know that Lucifer is a reality. One cannot understand our world unless one understands the existence of evil. A popular television analyst exposing a judge in Vermont who didn't give a sex offender prison time for abusing a child couldn't understand the judge's reasoning. It's rather simple. The judge doesn't believe in the existence of evil.

The analyst is to be commended for his vigilance in promoting justice. He, however, being raised in a Christian setting with a sense of right and wrong, is not fully knowledgeable on the conflict between the system out of which he has come and the teaching that we're all animals, with no purpose or direction. If one believes in determinism, the actions of another who is merely following natural instincts should not be punished. Those subscribing to such materialistic views believe there is no right and wrong. Morality simply has to do with cultural mores. A judge with that philosophy wouldn't think it appropriate to punish people. The corrective for sex offenders is reeducation. In this viewpoint, it's a matter of perspective so we'll condition people to function according to society's expectations.

One's worldview is vitally important in politics, the justice system, education, family settings, counseling, religion, the military, or any endeavor. People who don't believe in the existence of evil will take actions radically different than those who do. The results will range anywhere from the problematic to the catastrophic.

As with any subject, the nuances relating to a thing—in this case, how evil exists—are crucially significant. When I was a chaplain in the US Air Force, I had a chaplain friend who told me he believed in evil but not the Devil. He did use the Scripture as an authoritative resource in his teaching. I asked him how he explained the temptation of Jesus in Matthew 4:1–11. There Jesus had a personal encounter with the Devil as a real, specific, personal being. He reflected and replied, "I forgot about that. I'm going to have to reexamine what I believe about evil." He was an honest man but had been so influenced by our pervading materialistic viewpoint that he had forgotten about the source of evil.

Eve had a personal encounter with Lucifer. Eve's decision concerning her temptation and disobedience to God and that of Adam's are axiomatic to understanding what is happening in our world today, our individual destiny, and the future of mankind.

17

The Tree of Life

There was a special tree in the midst of Eden that captivated the interest of Adam. There has never been a tree on planet earth like it. It was called *the Tree of Life*. "In the middle of the garden were the tree of life and of the knowledge of good and evil" (Gen. 2:9 NIV).

Some, even among those who believe in God and the existence of Adam, take this tree to be a myth. One of the problems with that viewpoint is how does one determine what is myth and what is not myth? Someone has said those things that are problematic to readers of the Bible are like little pieces of onion skin. You peel off a piece and then there's more to peel, so you keep peeling until all you have left is the tears.

There are no myths in the Bible. The Bible is the product of God's Spirit. Myths are the inventions of mankind. As a youth I was taught that Christopher Columbus thought the world was flat. When Columbus sailed in 1492, his crew thought if they kept going they might sail off the earth. I later discovered that the prophet Isaiah two thousand years earlier through knowledge imparted to him by the Holy Spirit knew the earth was spherical. He wrote in Isaiah 40:22 that God sits "above the circle of the earth." When I visited Ephesus, a friend pointed out to me a similar representation. The statue of the Roman Emperor Trajan had the earth—as a circular globe—beneath his right foot. Under Trajan, in the first part of the second century, the Roman Empire reached its largest extent. The Romans knew in the second century that the shape of the earth was circular. I assume the ancients who studied cosmology, who were smarter than we think they were, understood the same. God who made the earth and inspired Isaiah in the writing of 40:22 certainly knew the shape of our planet.

Many who criticize the Bible have never read it. Some make fun of the idea of a Devil with horns and a long tail carrying a pitchfork. They, of course, are attacking medieval mythology, which has nothing to do with the Bible. I was disappointed when I read Bertrand Russell's book *Why I Am Not a Christian*. He didn't even consider the historic claims in the Bible relating to Jesus Christ, like His resurrection. I was later impressed by his daughter, a Christian, who criticized her father for not considering that information.

There is mythology. The gods of the myths, Jupiter, Zeus, Athena, and on and on, are no longer worshipped as major deities. They don't have contemporary temples. However billions of people on planet earth still believe in a Creator. Where there are imitations there is the genuine. Compare content in ancient myths with the account of Adam in the book of Genesis. You will see the difference.

In our resource, the Bible, there is a Tree of Life in Eden the beginning, and there is a future Tree of Life on the new earth in the New Jerusalem (Rev. 22:2). To understand the Scripture, my approach is to accept what is written in our resource. The Tree of Life was literal, not a sign or a symbol with some figurative meaning.

It's said that a person begins to die as soon as he or she is born.[64] Every individual has a life span calculated in years, months, days, hours, and

---

64 Augustine, translated by Rev. Marcus Dods, D.D., *The City of God, The Nicene and Post Nicene Fathers, Volume II, Saint Augustine*. (Grand Rapids, MI: Wm B. Eerdmans Publishing Company, 1979), 256, 249. Augustine taught the Tree of Life was a historic fact. Adam and Eve having access to the Tree of Life would live

minutes. It was not so with Adam. He did not start to die following his creation. If Adam had not sinned, though he existed in flesh, he would have lived forever. How often he ate of the Tree of Life we do not know. Strange as it seems, and totally foreign to our experience, the fruit of the Tree of Life assimilated by Adam worked in his body for his eternal health. Adam did not age. Adam and Eve stayed as they were. Without sin they would have continued in eternal youth.

In addition, one thoroughly studying God's purpose for Adam would know that He did not intend for Adam or humankind to live forever on planet earth. From the beginning God predetermined a future for mankind in Jesus Christ (Eph. 1:3–12). God knew before He created Adam what Adam was going to do. God knew you before you were born, and He knows, in His omniscience, what you will do all the days of your life (Ps. 139:16). God did not plan to have Adam live forever in human flesh. From the beginning it was predestinated that mankind would be celestial beings in God's royal family living forever in glory.

In our resource, it is clear that God started life on planet earth. In *The Case for a Creator* by Lee Strobel, especially chapter 6, "The Evidence of Physics," it is made crystal clear that life on planet earth did not just happen.[65] God gave Adam life, and God sustained his life. The Tree of Life, not figurative, in reality lets us know from the beginning, in Eden, life not only began by our Creator but is sustained by our Creator, Jesus Christ. The Creator equates to life. Without the Creator, there is no life.

---

forever. "And though they decayed not with years, nor drew nearer to death—a condition secured to them in God's marvelous grace by the tree of life, which grew along with the forbidden tree in the midst of the garden." Further, whether or not it was original with Augustine, he did teach that we begin to die as soon as we are born. Speaking of human kind "he begins to die as soon as he begins to live."

65 Lee Strobel, *The Case for a Creator*. (Grand Rapids, MI: Zondervan, 2004), 125–52.

18

The Tree of the Knowledge of Good and Evil

Yes, Adam had at his disposal, in the very midst of Eden, the Tree of Life. Also in the middle of the garden, at the center of everything, was the Tree of the Knowledge of Good and Evil. God told Adam that with one exception, he could eat of any tree in his garden. All the trees were created artistically beautiful (pleasant to the sight), and all the fruit on them was good to eat (Gen. 2:9). But the Tree of the Knowledge of Good and Evil was forbidden to Adam.

> God commanded the man [Adam] saying, "Of every tree of the garden you may freely eat; but of the tree of the knowledge of good and evil you shall not eat, for in the day that you eat of it you shall surely die." (Gen. 2:16–17)

It's possible that Adam saw animals die. They would not have eaten from the Tree of Life. Adam knew when he ate of the Tree of Life he would not die, but to eat of the forbidden fruit would cancel out the effect of the Tree of Life. Furthermore God had told Adam he would die "in the day" that he ate of it. The chronological order of Genesis 2 indicates Adam received his command not to eat of the forbidden fruit before Eve was created.

It is often suggested that the fruit on the Tree of the Knowledge of Good and Evil was an apple. Nowhere in the Bible is there a reference to the type of fruit on the tree.

Why did God have a tree such as the Tree of the Knowledge of Good and Evil? First it should be noted that God used this tree and the command not to eat of it to establish morality. There are things that are right, and there are things that are not right. Animals don't have morality. We observe in animals intelligence and mental capacities, but for the most part they do not have codes of conduct wherein they are expected to be morally responsible. God has built into humans a conscience about what is right and what is wrong. Furthermore God gave the Israelites a Law that contained a moral code that includes the Ten Commandments. The moral code as further defined by Jesus in the Sermon on the Mount (Matt. 5–7) gives input on the standard of righteousness that God requires of us. The true standard God requires of all mankind is the perfect life of Jesus Christ.

Second, on the Tree of the Knowledge of Good and Evil, the command not to eat of it, and the consequence, made it clear what God intended or purposed. God made mankind to be free. Adam was free not to eat of the forbidden fruit or he could eat and suffer the penalty. God wants people to love Him and worship Him because they choose to do so.

We don't know what was happening in the heavens after earth was created concerning Lucifer's revolt. However, we do know that Satan came to planet earth, and through his person evil was present. But as far as we know, before Adam and Eve partook of the forbidden fruit of the Tree of the Knowledge of Good and Evil, evil had no influence or effect on planet earth or on Adam and Eve. Evil, however, did exist. If Adam and Eve were to serve God, it was inevitable that they would have to choose good that is God and not evil. Not only did Adam need to serve God and not Satan, but Adam also needed to choose differently than Satan had chosen. Adam and humankind were created to worship God, to be loyal. On Satan and his rebellion, it was important there be no repeat. Adam and humankind were not to be like Satan. God would require faith (trust) in the Son of God for His people.

Because there was a Tree of the Knowledge of Good and Evil does not necessitate dualism. Some would interject you cannot do good or know good unless you know evil.

God is holy! God says, "Be holy, because I am holy" (1 Peter 1:16 NIV). God is set apart or separate from sin, that which is impure. God is morally whole and perfect. God has no evil in Him. He made the world good. You do not have to know evil to be good. Good exists without evil. Adam and Eve had knowledge of good. All they did was good, and all they experienced was good. There was no evil in them. There would be no evil for Adam and Eve until they ate of the forbidden fruit giving them knowledge of evil. Evil did exist, but Adam and Eve did not know evil.

Eating of the Tree of the Knowledge of Good and Evil was in itself evil. God is just (Acts 3:14), perfectly reasonable, fair, good, and upright in all He does or requires. Adam was created by God. Adam was given friendship and fellowship. Adam received a beautiful environment filled with wonderment—having all kinds of amazing animal and plant life. Adam was sustained daily by the love of God, a benevolent Overseer. Adam was given a beautiful wife who was comparable to him. He had Eve and Eve had him, each having another human, an intimate horizontal relationship, a unique and supernatural gift from heaven. Adam didn't have a long list of things he couldn't do. He had one commandment—don't eat of the forbidden fruit.

Adam didn't need the fruit that was on the Tree of the Knowledge of Good and Evil. To eat would be to disobey God. Adam didn't have to eat of the forbidden fruit. He had the power of choice—the power not to eat. Evidently for some time—it could have been eons, we don't know—Adam did not eat.

Last of all, concerning the Tree of the Knowledge of Good and Evil, why did God have the right to command Adam not to eat? God created Adam and Eve. The earth is the Lord's and all that is upon it (Ps. 24:1). God did not create Adam to be a slave. God created Adam and his posterity for great dignity and honor. God made Adam, a being in His image, for glory (Isa. 43:6–7). God intended mankind to be His sons and daughters, to reign with Him in heavenly realms. Adam could not, however, fulfill the purpose for which God created him unless he was willing to acknowledge God for who He is, take his rightful place in worshipping Him, and obey Him in the arrangement God had for his life.

19

The Temptation

In Genesis 3:1–6, Eve was tempted to eat of the fruit on the Tree of the Knowledge of Good and Evil. Eve succumbed to temptation and ate. She gave to Adam, and he ate. Both Adam and Eve disobeyed God's command not to eat.

Eve was led to disobedience, deceived by the serpent, namely Satan, in the body of a snake. We've already noted Adam and Eve could communicate with the animals in Eden. Eve seemed to think it normal that she could speak to the serpent at the Tree of the Knowledge of Good and Evil and the serpent could speak to her. As we will note later (see chapter 21, "The Promise"), the serpent that deceived Eve, was different than any serpent on our planet today.

Eve was led astray by a Tempter. Lucifer, Satan, and the Devil, all the same person, is called the Tempter in Matthew 4:3. It is important to understand that God tempts no one. God tests, but He does not tempt. Each person who sins and is disobedient to God does so out of his or her own lust or desire to get whatever it is Satan is offering as an inducement to sin (James 1:13–14).

One way the goodness of God is manifest is in His providence to deliver us from temptation. The apostle Paul wrote,

> No temptation has overtaken you except such as is common to man: but God is faithful, who will not allow you to be tempted beyond what you are able, but with the temptation will also make the way of escape, that you may be able to bear it. (1 Cor. 10:13)

What was Eve's way of escape? It was Adam. Julius Caesar copied an excellent military strategy from Satan. He divides and conquers. There were only two humans on planet earth. The absolute worst decision Eve could have made to mess up was to eat the forbidden fruit. The choice to eat was of such a magnitude that she should have consulted her husband before running up a bill she could not pay. But Satan appealed to Eve alone. We don't know how many times he talked to her. It appears Eve made a unilateral decision, and that was her undoing.

We have words in Genesis 3:1–6 describing what happened in the temptation. First the serpent attacked God. His attack was cunning, disguised as an innocent question, pretending to have Eve's best interest at heart yet implying that God was short changing her. Satan asked, "Has God indeed said, You shall not eat of every tree of the garden?" (Gen. 3:1). In other words, God has kept something from you. You can't eat of every tree of the garden. The truth is God gave Adam and Eve all the trees in the garden, everything, including their lives, a relationship with Him, and freedom. The only thing Adam and Eve did not have was on one tree, the Knowledge of Good and Evil, or in reality, evil.

Eve replied they could eat fruit from the trees in the garden, but God did say, "You must not eat fruit from the tree that is in the middle of the garden, and you must not touch it, or you will die" (Gen. 3:3 NIV)

We don't know if God spoke to Eve about this or if she got her information solely from Adam. Eve, however, was not exact. She said they were not to eat of the tree in the middle of the garden. The truth is there were two trees in Eden's midst. They could eat of one of them—that is the Tree of Life. Adam and Eve had a choice—it was life or death. We have the same choice.

What did God withhold from Adam and Eve? The answer is the knowledge of evil. More than one person has told me, "Knowledge is power." It's good to acquire knowledge. It is also significant to understand that no one is being short changed when they don't have the knowledge of evil. Those using their knowledge of evil for power do a horrendous amount of damage—to themselves, others, and planet earth.

The Devil wanted Eve to think she was denied Eden's best—the fruit in the middle of the garden. We know Eve had the Tree of Life—fruit in the midst of the garden. But of the forbidden fruit, Eve told the serpent they could not eat it or touch it lest they die. Now God had not said, "Don't touch it." It appears that Adam told Eve about the tree, and to ensure she didn't eat the fruit, he probably added, "Don't touch it." Adam may have reasoned if Eve didn't touch it, she wouldn't eat it.

Then the serpent's deception took a new turn. This second deception was a blatant lie. He said, "You will not surely die" (Gen. 3:4 NIV). This is called the "lie" in Romans 1:25. The idea—there is no death. Things just "are." The creation becomes the Creator. As noted earlier, the concept that everything just happened is not new. The greatest mythology Satan has ever fostered on mankind is the myth that everything just is. Continuing on, third, Satan cast further aspersion against God. He said, "For God knows that when you eat of it your eyes will be opened, and you will be like God, knowing good and evil" (Gen. 3:5 NIV). Here we have a half truth. If Eve ate of the fruit, she would know not only good but she would know evil. The main falsehood was that Eve would be like God. Eve knew there was a God because she talked with Him. But her chief temptation was to be her own god.

There you have it. Man's biggest problem is the desire to be God. Lucifer tempted Eve with his own obsession. He said,

> I will ascend into heaven, I will exalt my throne above the
> stars of God; I will sit on the mount of the congregation
> On the further sides of the north; I will ascend above

the heights of the clouds, I will be like the Most High. (Isa. 14:13–14)

John Milton in his classic, *Paradise Lost*, presents Satan as a being of revenge, immortal hate, who will never submit or yield to God. He will never bow or sue for grace. Satan says, "Better to reign in hell, than to serve in heaven." His aim is to pervert the creation of God on planet earth. Never actually do good is his practice and that of the fallen angels he rules. His strategy is, "Out of good still to find means of evil."[66]

So Satan hooked Eve, like one would catch a prize fish with cunningly devised attractive bait. The "Be your own God" lure he used from the beginning. Current world history books begin with prehistory, carefully sketching how man evolved out of the elements, an idea totally out of date and radically inconsistent with modern scientific knowledge (read *The Case for a Creator* by Lee Strobel). That's a major part of Satan's deception. You will not (really) surely die. Get rid of God. Make everything natural. You're just a blob of chemicals, matter that ages and goes back to the dust. Accept death; there is no beyond.

The central strategy, continuing on, is that you can be your own god or a god. In early Sumer, the first era of history, there was worship with priests. The priests were the ruling class who accumulated wealth through exploitation of labor and the imposition of taxes. The ruler is the chief priest.[67] In the mythology of that time, we learn the chief priest represented the gods. He and other priests assumed quasi-divine status.[68] This arrangement would continue through ancient history, right on down to the Roman Empire. I've already briefly alluded to it. An additional illustration, about how people thought they could be a god, is

---

66 John Milton, *Paradise Lost, Britannica, Great Books, Volume 32*. (Chicago: Encyclopedia Britannica, Inc., 1988), 93–99.

67 Geoffrey Parker, *Compact History of the World*. (London: Harper Collins Publishers, 2008), 20–21.

68 Arthur Cotterell, *World Mythology*. (Bath, UK: Parragon Publishing, 1999), 15.

the Emperor Hadrian, who has his young lover, Antinous, who drowned while swimming, deified, and a cluster of stars named after him.[69]

There is then this attraction to be one's own god—to be god or a god. In this case, there is amorality. A person ends up making his or her own rules. Pandemonium results, with the survival of the fittest.[70] Type-A people reach for the stars regardless of the consequences. Other people are stepping stones one uses to get to the top. Academicians create pockets of snobbery and are recognized as the experts who alone possess the proper way—their own relative truth. Politicians become a law unto themselves, as the elite who determine who has what and how we should live. And all have a strong inclination to live their lives in step with the famous song of Frank Sinatra, *I Did It My Way.* See Mark 14:35–36.

"When the woman saw that the fruit of the tree was good for food, and pleasing to the eye, and desirable for gaining wisdom, she took some and ate it" (Gen. 3:6 NIV). Eve didn't listen to God. Eve didn't listen to her husband. Eve became a harbinger of those who ignore, oppose, malign, and despise God's Word. Eve was deceived, so in eating she chose evil.

The apostle John warns us not to love the world rather than the Father—God. He specifies what he means: "For all that is in the world—the lust

---

69 Michael Kerrigan, *A Dark History: The Roman Emperors.* (New York: Metro Books, 2008), 155–7. Hadrian's favorite was not a priest. The point is Hadrian had his lover deified—declared a god. From ancient times men sought special status for themselves and others they wished to single out as those above the law and other human beings. This is exactly why Eve ate of the forbidden fruit and led Adam into doing the same. They sought god status. They claimed deity rather than humanity. Dictators and the like do the same even if they don't publicly seek deification. Those who blatantly live without God by their lifestyle declare they don't need God. They are their own god, gods unto themselves.

70 John Milton, Mortimer J. Adler, Associate Editor, *Paradise Lost,* Britannica, Great Books, Volume 32. (Chicago: Encyclopedia Britannic, Inc., 1988), 93, 110. Pandemonium is a word coined by John Milton in his classic *Paradise Lost.* A place of tumult, it was the capitol of hell. Confusion and destruction happens in society, on planet earth, when people revolt against their Creator and seek to live without Him.

of the flesh, the lust of the eyes, and the pride of life—is not of the Father but the world" (1 John 2:16).

We are tempted to sin by desiring things to gratify the flesh, wanting what looks appealing and pursuing that which satisfies our pride and is inflating to our ego. In all these cases, there are specifics that God clearly declares evil. Succumbing to the lust of the flesh, the lust of the eyes, and the pride of life, forbidden fruit as referenced in the Word of God puts us at odds with God. Eve had more than she could eat of the most delectable food imaginable. She wanted more. She was not satisfied, thankful. (See Romans 1:18–21, "Nor were thankful"). She looked and had to have. She wanted to be God. In eating she rejected God. God became dead to her. She became acquainted with evil. In essence her act communicated, "God, I want you out of my life." God doesn't force Himself on anyone. Eve's disobedience said, "I can make it on my own. I don't need you." God's response was, "Okay, have a go at it. See how you make out."

Adam with Eve then partook. "She also gave some to her husband, who was with her, and he ate it." It looks like Eve chose to partake of the forbidden fruit when Adam was present. Eve did not include Adam in her decision but did want him to accompany her in disobedience. (Gen. 3:6 NIV). Regardless of what Adam wanted she picked a fruit and ate it. There it was done. Adam in shock stood by watching. Eve picked another fruit, handed it to Adam and he ate. That's how the psychology of sin works.

Adam was not deceived (1 Tim. 2:14).Why did Adam eat? We don't know. Adam, it seems, succumbing to an unhealthy love chose to share Eve's fate. Adam chose loyalty to his wife rather than God. In so doing, he too chose evil, and in the process, he too disobeyed God. It's something people do every day—choose race rather than truth, family rather than justice, and agenda rather than good. Adam and Eve both died the moment they disobeyed God.

20

The Fall

Adam saw Eve had lost her aura. She was naked. He saw Eve naked for the first time. As indicated, it may have been out of shock and a false sense of loyalty he partook of the forbidden fruit. Eve saw Adam was naked. They individually recognized their beautiful glow had extinguished. "The eyes of both of them were open, and they realized they were naked" (Gen. 3:7 NIV). (They were not like God, gods! Eve realized Satan had lied. All the Devil's apples have worms.)

The nakedness of Adam and Eve was now *erom* nakedness (see chapter 10 to refresh your understanding of erom nakedness). The nakedness after eating the forbidden fruit was one of shame. In his disobedience to God, man not only lost glory; he descended to shame. This in one aspect would later come to be seen in the Far East as losing face—dishonor.

Adam's transgression is called sin. Sin is real. It is something. It's the poison of the forbidden fruit. In eating, man became spiritually ill. Adam's choice brought disease to his own spirit. The malady now affecting Adam did so in his intellect (mental health), psychologically - his emotional wholeness, his physical wellbeing, his length of life, and relationally. Sin produces death (1 Cor. 15:56). Death is separation from God. Adam and Eve did not physically die on the day they ate of the forbidden fruit. But they did die. Their relationship with God was ruptured. They had a change of status. They had been in intimate fellowship. As soon as they ate, they became estranged. Their physical life span would be shortened. The terribleness of death is experienced in separation. When a loved one's spirit departs, that person is no longer on planet earth.

When Adam and Eve became naked, knew they were naked, and understood they were naked, "They sewed fig leaves together and made coverings for themselves" (Gen. 3:7 NIV). Later other people would go naked. Whether such folk did so innocently or not I do not know. Their sexual practices would illustrate innocence or non-innocence. Those who reject God usually have no criticism in regard to how other people live or what anyone does when it comes to sexual relations.

Adam and Eve knew what was done and immediately saw they lost something. Their feelings were of guilt. There are two kinds of guilt: legitimate guilt and false guilt. False guilt is when guilt is self-generated. People who have false guilt feel bad about something when they shouldn't feel bad about it. False guilt is self-imposed by faulty thinking.

Then there is legitimate guilt. Legitimate guilt is when we feel bad about something because we have violated the law of God. Adam and Eve introduced guilt to the human race. They felt guilty because they were guilty of breaking God's commandment not to eat of the fruit of the Knowledge of the Tree of Good and Evil. The first response to guilt was to cover it up, denial. They tried to makes clothes of fig leaves. (We have knowledge here of one kind of fruit in the garden. Maybe the fruit on the Tree of the Knowledge of Good and Evil was figs.)

Adam and Eve could not do for themselves what God had given them with His aura. They heard God walking in the garden in the cool of the day, probably in the evening. God was calling for them, so Adam and Eve tried to hide among trees (Gen. 3:8). Here we have another psychological illness—avoidance.

God called to them, "Where are you?" (Gen. 3:9 NIV). God knew where they were, and He knew what they had done. God wanted them to fess up. He wants us to be honest, not wear masks and pretend to be something we are not. Fig leaves cannot hide our nakedness.

Adam called out, "I heard you in the garden, and I was afraid because I was naked; so I hid" (Gen. 3:10 NIV). Having heard God calling for them, Adam and Eve hid. Adam's pronoun was not "we" but "I." Was Adam exercising spiritual leadership, or was he embarrassed, having broken God's commandment, jettisoning Eve? Another factor stemming out of the fall was fear. Adam said, "I was afraid." So Adam "hid himself."

God's reply was, "Who told you that you were naked? Have you eaten from the tree of that I commanded you not to eat from?" (Gen. 3:11 NIV). The first step toward restitution is to admit one's transgression.

Adam's response was to make an excuse. Here we have the beginning of the blame game. Adam said, "The woman you put here with me - she gave me some fruit from the tree, and I ate" (Gen. 3:12 NIV). For whatever reason Adam ate of the forbidden fruit, in the presence of God, he morally collapsed.

Note, another effect of sin was that Adam for the moment became bitter against God. When one breaks God's law, it leads to a spirit of hostility against God. Otherwise Adam's response to God's question, "Have you eaten from the tree I commanded that you should not eat?" was to insinuate, "It was the woman you gave me that led to this. Things were fine until Eve arrived. It was you and me, God. Then you gave me this woman—and look what happened. It was the woman you gave me." Thus in a round-about way, Adam accused God, blamed God for his sin.

Adam was condemned. He condemned himself when he ate of the fruit. Nevertheless, God's practice is to give the guilty party opportunity to talk about it and to admit one's guilt. Adam failed, having no excuse for his disobedience, which was a rejection of the Creator and His law. Now it was Eve's turn.

God turned to the woman, "What is this you have done?" The woman answered "The serpent deceived me, and I ate" (Gen. 3:13 NIV). Eve told the truth. Nevertheless, Eve too was playing the blame game. How sad! Eve knew immediately when she lost her aura that she had been deceived.

God then turned to the serpent. God asked no question of the serpent. God told the woman and the serpent (Satan) that which He determined for mankind. We'll examine that separately under the chapter titled "Promise." It's appropriate here to remember who God is. Adam and Eve momentarily forgot. The people of Judah did the same in the time of Isaiah. Many of us today need to be reminded. The Creator, Jesus, the Son of God, says,

> I am God, and there is no other; I am God, there is none like Me, Declaring the end from the beginning, And from ancient times things that are not done, Saying, My counsel shall stand, And I will do all My pleasure. (Isa. 46:9–10)

This is what we'll see in Genesis 3:15. God will declare in the beginning, to Adam and Eve, what He is going to do.

Adam and Eve now had low self-esteem. There are Christians who debunk the idea of low self-esteem, thinking it is an idea foisted on us that has no merit or basis in reality. Low self-esteem, however, has to do with not feeling good about self because something is wrong. Something is wrong with us. It's called sin. The human race got it from Adam's disobedience. When a person is born, he or she inherits Adam's sinful nature. No individual is held accountable for Adam's sin, but soon by choice every person sins, thus alienating self from God. We are a fallen race.

Adam and Eve's sin destroyed their relationship with God. Their sin put them at odds with each other. Individually sin changed how each person felt about self. These conditions passed on to all mankind. We'll see further effects of eating the forbidden fruit when we look at the curse God put on Adam and Eve and the earth. We'll see still further the effect sin has on the family and the relationship people have with each other. The effects of Satan, sin, and death are all results of Adam and Eve's fall. Studying Adam and sin's beginning in Eden clarifies our experience and fits perfectly with knowledge we have about ourselves, life on earth.

21

The Promise

Adam's worst day occurred when he ate of the forbidden fruit. Putting it in perspective, Adam's worst day became the worst day in the history of the human race. Up until that time, every day for Adam was a wonderful day. Adam's disobedience got him tossed out of Eden, brought him shame and sadness, and resulted in horrendous adversity, suffering, and bereavement for all mankind. God, however, is a God of goodness and grace. Immediately God gave Adam and all mankind a promise.

God cursed the serpent. The serpent went through a physiological change. He had walked upright and was a creature of beauty. Henceforth he would crawl on his belly. People the world over would fear his progeny. And to (the serpent) Satan and Eve, God said, "And I will put enmity Between you and the woman, And between your seed and her Seed; He shall bruise your head, And you shall bruise His heel" (Gen. 3:15).

Death entered mankind. But God would destroy the work of the Devil and death. Genesis 3:15 is a promised deliverance through Jesus Christ. Jesus is the "He" that would bruise the serpent's head. The "He" promised to Eve, and to all mankind, would be born of a woman. A woman led the world into sin and death. A woman would bear the man through whom the world would be rescued—saved. The specific woman who would birth the coming Deliverer, the Savior of mankind and the world, would be the virgin, Mary (Isa. 7:14, Matt. 1:23).

God said He would put enmity between the serpent and the woman. The war between God and Lucifer that began in celestial realms now came to planet earth. The warfare would be between the serpent and his seed, Lucifer and his fallen angels, and the woman and her seed, humankind and God, Jesus Christ, the promised "He."

Satan would bruise mankind's heel. Allegorically, just as a serpent or poisonous snake bites an individual's heel, when that person walks by, so Satan would afflict mankind with suffering, pain, and death. The specific Seed out of a woman, of mankind, that would fight against the Devil and his angels is Jesus Christ. The Son of God would work through humankind against the forces of evil on earth until being born as a man, Jesus. Then He would defeat the serpent, smash its head, and destroy death, the effect of sin.

God made Adam the steward of planet earth. We don't know the boundaries established by God as to what Satan can and cannot do in his insurrection against God. In the book of Job Satan appears with the sons of God (angels) in God's presence (Job 1:6). We know from verse 7 that Satan is busy going to and fro on the earth, walking back and forth on it. Satan was allowed to torment Job, but Satan had limits on what he could and could not do. In Job we see behind the scene. We learn it is the Devil, Lucifer, who afflicts us.

We don't know why Satan is allowed to do what he does. Hugh Grotius, a Dutch theologian who laid the foundation for international law, developed what is known as the governmental view of the atonement.[71] His view has

---

71 Winston Walker, *A History of the Christian Church.* (New York: Charles Scribner's Sons, 1959), 401. Grotius's contribution, "an important theory of the atonement," provides food for thought in calling to our attention the need to have law for the purpose of justice but it, according to Winston Walker, falls short by denying the need of the payment of penalty. "Christ died, not for general justice, but for me."

Jesus reconciling us to God by operating within a framework of law God established to rule the universe by justice. Grotius's perspective makes a great deal of sense, especially when we apply it to the operation of Satan and the reason God allows him to do what he does. Our resource on Adam, the Scripture, teaches us Satan's time of operation is limited. Satan will be brought to justice. In the meantime, Adam's disobedience to God brought him and our planet under the influence of Lucifer. When Adam ate of the forbidden fruit, he chose Satan rather than God. The apostle John wrote, "The whole world is under the control of the evil one" (1 John 5:19 NIV). Jesus identified Satan as the ruler of this world (John 14:30).

The promise of God in Genesis 3:15 had to do with the coming of Jesus Christ and the reversal of the predicament caused by Adam's disobedience. "For by one man's disobedience [Adam's] many were made sinners, so also by one Man's obedience [Jesus] many will be made righteous" (Rom. 5:19). "For as in Adam all die, even so in Christ all will be made alive" (that is all who are in Christ will have immortality) (1 Cor. 15:22 NIV).

22

Curses

Adam, created in the image of God, was superior to the animal creation. He was put in the garden to tend it and keep it (Gen. 2:15). Adam himself was a created being subject to his Creator. Having disobeyed his Creator, Adam received the penalty of death. The Creator, who is holy and just (Acts 3:14), has determined the way to deal with disobedience is by punishment. At the same time, the Creator is benevolent and gracious. On the day Adam ate of the forbidden fruit, he died; that is, he became estranged in his relationship to God. The same day God's love was manifested in the promise of Genesis 3:15. God does not make threats. God instructed Adam about the consequences of disobedience. When Adam fell, he died, but God immediately gave hope and a way of reconciliation.

Part of the fall of Adam and the impending penalty of death had to do with resulting curses. Following the information we have in Genesis 3:15, God continued in conversation with Eve. To the woman He said, "I will greatly multiple your sorrow and your conception; in pain you shall bring forth children. Your desire shall be for your husband, and he shall rule over you" (Gen. 3:16).

Thus women would have difficulty in bearing children. It would involve pain and in many cases complications, some resulting in the death of the child or children. A woman's desire would be for her husband. The idea in Hebrew is that women would seek to dominate men. This of course leads to manipulation and all sorts of unhealthy relationships. Men would also rule women or be given to male chauvinism. It's not that God would distress women but that without God in mankind's lives and His blessedness, the presence of Satan and sin would lead to the abuse and misuse of women.

God, having spoken to Satan and the woman, Eve, then spoke to Adam.

> To Adam He said: "Because you have heeded the voice of your wife, and have eaten from the tree of which I commanded you, saying, 'You shall not eat of it: Cursed is the ground for your sake; in toil you shall eat of it All the days of your life. Both thorns and thistles it shall bring forth for you, And you shall eat the herb of the field, In the sweat of your face you shall eat bread Till you return to the ground, for out of it you were taken; For dust you are, And to the dust you shall return" (Gen. 3:17–19)

God found fault with Adam for listening to his wife instead of honoring his Creator and the command not to eat from the tree God had clearly declared off limits. The application, as already emphasized in chapter 7, "Husband," is that our priority relationship is with our Creator, God, and that our obedience must be to Him. This priority was taught by Jesus Christ: "But seek first his kingdom and his righteousness and all these things [what we eat and what we wear] will be given to you as well" (Matt. 6:33 NIV).

Adam was told the ground, or the earth, was now cursed. In the garden God brought forth fruit and plant life to be used for food in abundance— gratis. Now the ground would produce thorns and thistles (all sorts of weeds). Adam would have to labor to have success with gardening. All things would come through the sweat of his face. Life would be difficult, there would be suffering.

Although Adam died the moment he ate of the Tree of the Knowledge of Good and Evil, he did not experience the terribleness of death until the separation that takes place when a person physically dies. The grave effectively communicates the horribleness of death in the physical finality of a person's departure. "For dust you are and to dust you will return." (Gen. 3:19 NIV)

The relational curses against Adam and Eve, however, are to be ameliorated in Christian conversion and sanctification through Jesus Christ. Part of God's curse against Adam and Eve in Genesis 3:16 are currently in the process of elimination. Separated from God, a woman's desire would be toward her husband—that is, a wife would seek to control her husband. The husband would seek to rule over his wife—that is, to see the feminine as inferior and women as possessions or objects to keep oppressed.

Liberation, the change in the relationship between a husband and wife, comes with the fulfillment of the promised in Genesis 3:15. Through Jesus, the promised Seed who smacked the serpent in the head, the relationship of a husband and a wife is in the process of Edenic restoration. As a born-again person with new life, a wife learns not to seek control of her husband but to honor him by having a proper spirit toward him. The husband learns to love his wife with a proper respect toward her (Eph. 5:17–33). Thus true Christianity liberates women. A wife is now understood to be a woman comparable to a man (Gen. 2:20). A husband and wife, co-equal, working together as partners in life are to fulfill their God given task on planet earth.

23

Clothing

Adam and Eve were naked. Part of their condition had to do with shame. Their shame had to do with guilt and embarrassment for disobeying God. God clothed them to cover their nakedness. They needed to be clothed to be in the presence of God. Being clothed indicated their sin would be removed and they would receive righteousness. Being clothed meant restoration.

"Also for Adam and his wife the Lord God made tunics of skin, and clothed them" (Gen. 3:21). Genesis 3:21 is the first passage of Scripture following Genesis 3:15 prefiguring the salvation God would provide for Adam, Eve, and their posterity through Jesus Christ.

God made Adam and Eve tunics of skin. A tunic is a slip-on garment with sleeves or sleeveless that is knee length or longer. The tunics to cover Adam and Eve's nakedness were made of skins taken from animals.

Three factors may be seen in the garments of skins. First, they were skins of animals. Animals were slain to provide the skins that clothed Adam and Eve. In the slaying of animals, blood was shed. This theme, started with Adam and Eve, would continue through the Old Testament in Scripture, our resource, until the one to whom it pointed, Jesus Christ, died on the cross, giving His blood, His life, to take away our sin and restore us to God. Those who study the history of mankind will note that those who proceed from Adam and Eve, mankind, throughout history used blood sacrifice in their worship. The Bible teaches that we are reconciled to God—brought back to an okay relationship with God—through the blood of Jesus Christ. Speaking of Jesus Christ, the apostle Paul wrote, "In him we have redemption through His blood, the forgiveness of sins, in accordance with the riches of God's grace" (Eph. 1:7 NIV).

Second, the provision of skins for Adam and Eve was vicarious. Vicarious means it was done for them. Adam and Eve did not get the skins for themselves. The Scripture indicates God made the tunics of skin and clothed Adam and Eve. In salvation, getting back into a right relationship with God is through the sacrifice Jesus Christ made for us through His death on the cross, His burial, and His resurrection. "We also rejoice in God though our Lord Jesus Christ, through whom we have now received reconciliation" (Rom. 5:11 NIV).

Third, the clothing of Adam and Eve is a picture of being clothed with the righteousness of Jesus Christ. Jeremiah in the Old Testament prophesied about the coming Messiah, calling Him, "The Lord Our Righteousness" (Jer. 23:6 NIV). Jesus alone, the Messiah, without sin (2 Cor. 5:20–21), met the standard (righteousness) required by God to be in a relationship with Him (as a man on earth) and to go to heaven. He is the righteousness of God (Rom. 1:16–17). When a person believes in Jesus Christ, the Son of God, that person receives the righteousness of God as a free gift (Rom. 3:21–22). Ultimately, because we are clothed spiritually with the righteousness of Christ, we are clothed through Christ with a new body. Thus we will not be naked (2 Cor. 5:1–8).

Adam and Eve being clothed by God indicates that they believed in God and His promise (which is salvation through Jesus Christ). "And without faith it is impossible to please God, because anyone who comes to him must believe that he exists, and that he rewards those who earnestly seek Him" (Heb. 11:6 NIV).

24

Expulsion

Adam is a precursor to what happens to mankind with loss and suffering. Adam lost his perfect standing with God. He lost his exalted position in the garden. Like many who have moral failures and are forced to resign, Adam retired in disgrace. Eve, as Adam's wife, shared in his downgrade. For the first time in their lives, Adam and Eve knew what it meant to cry—have tears. They were real people. Surely they wept. And we too, as we learn their story, must weep. We weep for them, we weep for mankind, we weep for creation, and we weep for ourselves.

> Then the Lord God said, "Behold, the man has become like one of us, to know good and evil, And now, lest he put out his hand and take also of the tree of life, and eat, and live forever"—therefore the Lord God sent him out of the garden of Eden to till the ground from which he was taken. So he drove out the man; and He placed cherubim at the east of the garden of Eden, and a flaming sword which turned every way to guard the way to the tree of life. (Gen. 3:22–24)

Adam was the son of God, a special created being made in His image (Luke 3:38). He lost that relationship temporarily (during the days of his life on planet earth). He would get his status back by faith in the Son of God—Jesus

Christ. Adam would be a son once again in his future life by faith. "You are all sons of God through faith in Christ Jesus" (Gal. 3:26 NIV).[72]

Adam was a vagabond for some time. His expulsion was the first flux of human dispersions from one area to another throughout the history of mankind. Having lost his original home, Eden, the garden, he set the trend for Abraham some twenty generations later. Adam and Eve were now strangers and pilgrims on earth (Heb. 11:13–16). We are all strangers and pilgrims seeking a heavenly country, some better place to call home (a perfect place). The spot we seek is not here but somewhere beyond the blue.

God did not want man to live forever in a physical body. God created every person with certain designs. First, a person would live forever. Second, a person is to live in heaven, a celestial place. Third, a person is created for glory. Christ died to bring us to glory (Heb. 2:10). All these designs are to be combined.

The eternal glory (2 Cor. 4:17) God intends for us is to live with Him in a celestial realm, heaven (1 Cor. 15:45–49), forever in a celestial body— one like that of the risen Christ (2 Cor. 5:1).

---

72 There is a difference between Adam as the son of God, the only begotten Son of God, and the sons of God being redeemed in creation. Adam, the son of God, was created by God in the image of God, the first human being, a man of flesh and blood, perfect before the fall, a unique person, who lived on planet earth for 930 years before he physically died. He was not divine. The only begotten Son of God who we know as Jesus Christ is divine and eternally God (John 1:18). The apostle John refers to Jesus as the only begotten Son, the preexistent one who teaches us about God the Father. This is the Son Who was sent by the Father and became flesh and blood, incarnate, born as a human (John 1:14). Jesus is the Word Who was with God, and is God, Who created all things (John 1:1–2). Jesus, the only begotten Son of God, totally unique, is fully God and fully man. Human beings, creatures who are born again, on the other hand, are adopted as sons of God into the family of God through Jesus Christ (1 John 3:1–3, Rom. 8:23). People prior to the death of Jesus on the cross and after the death of Jesus, who looked to Him as the Son of God, become children of God or sons of God by faith (Heb. 9:15, Gal. 3:26). As sons and daughters of God, they are in the family of God and have special glory but are not gods and will not ever be gods.

Adam and Eve, expelled from Eden, were to till the ground, to farm (Gen. 3:23). Temporarily they went east. A cherubim, heavenly being, angel, was stationed at the east of the garden to keep them from returning to eat of the Tree of Life. How long the Tree of Life remained we do not know. It is lost to us, as is the location of Eden.

After thirteen generations, the civilization of Sumer and its city states emerged in the Fertile Crescent, followed by the same kind of society in Egypt.[73] We note the people in these settlements were highly intelligent.[74] Humankind was aware of God and creation. Early leaders wanted to be like gods or be gods so they could do their own thing.[75]

---

73 Genesis 5 and 10 provide thirteen generations from Adam to Nimrod, the great-grandson of Noah who founded Babel, Erech, Accad, and Calneh, cities in the area of Sumer, where the written history of man begins (Gen. 10:1, 6–12). This would be the time frame of the great-great-great-great-great-grandfather of Abraham (Gen. 11–12).

74 Anton Gill, *The Rise and Fall of Babylon, Gateway of The Gods*. (New York: Metro Books, 2008). "The Greatest of the Babylonian astronomers, Kidinnu, who was active in the second half of the fourth century BC was able to calculate the duration of the solar year with an error of only 4 minutes and 32.65 seconds. This calculation was fractionally more accurate than that of the Czech astronomer Theodor von Oppolzer (1841-86) in a posthumously published work of 1887. The fact that Kidinnu reached such a result at all is impressive, but his achievements should be measured against a scientific tradition that dates back to Sumerian times." Gill also notes, concerning the sciences, "Several of the discoveries we usually attribute to the ancient Greeks, such as Pythagoras' theorem and the Archimedes screw, were in fact of Babylonian origin." These ancient people were not nut gathers. In fact, history teaches nothing about nut gathering except what is known concerning some aborigines a few centuries ago.

75 Susan Wise Bauer, *The History of the Ancient World*. (New York: W.W. Norton & Company, Inc., 2007). The first kingships in Sumer, pre-flood, descended from heaven (3). There were eight kings before the Sumer account of the flood (4). Kingship was a gift from the gods (7). The fifth king on the Sumerian list, Dumuzi, had the blood of the gods in his veins (8). There are, by the way, mixed in with the information we have about leaders claiming godhood, stories of the flood in the accounts of Sumer and also from the Babylonians, the Egyptians, from Genesis, the Hebrews, India, the Chinese, and Americas with the Mayans and Incas (10–17). The first dynasty of pharaohs became gods (61). "The early pharaohs of Egypt claimed to be the earthly embodiment of Horus the permanent ruler of the sky, born from the goddess Isis" (65). Anton Gill, Ibid., Naram-Sin, who ruled 2254

25

Earth Change

Adam's experience concerning earth change can be summed up by the title *Paradise Lost*, the book written by John Milton. There are two specific biblical periods in which we know there was earth change. Most people understand there were changes to our planet through the universal flood in the days of Noah. For example, before the flood, Noah had never experienced rain. Genesis 2:5 states, "The Lord God had not caused it to rain on the earth." In Adam's time we are taught the earth was watered by a mist—water that came up from the earth, not water coming down from the atmosphere. In Genesis 2:6 we read, "A mist went up from the earth and watered the whole face of the ground."

In Noah's travail, God caused it to rain on the earth forty days and forty nights (Gen. 7:4). Noah and his family experienced atmospheric

---

to 2218 BC in the Akkadian Empire, conferred godhood upon himself (35–37). Gudea of Lagash (2141–2122 BC) elevated himself to godhead (38). Shulgi of the third dynasty of Ur assumed godhead, claiming divine descent (38–40). The pharaohs of Egypt were gods incarnate, the humbler subjects forbidden to look at them (52). "From the great Amorite king Hammurabi to the last Babylonian king of all, Nabonidus, a period spanning over one thousand years, kings always claimed to have received their remit from the gods" (52). "According to general Mesopotamian tradition (going back to the first writings in history, in Sumer), the king was viewed as the god's ... earthy representative" (76).

changes. This is what our resource, the Scripture, teaches and has taught for thousands of years. It means, of course, that radiation activity in the upper atmosphere has not been constant in the production of carbon 14. Long before there was any process of carbon dating used to give various dates for fossils, our data on Adam places limitations on its accuracy in some measurements. Atmospheric changes, different from conditions in Eden, would eventuate into hurricanes, tornadoes, and the kind of weather conditions we experience in our own time. Also from the days of Noah there would not only be rain storms and floods but also droughts and various other climatic changes. There were changes to and from an ice age.

In addition, the fact that the earth was covered by water during the great deluge obviously brought about geographical changes. One may have been the submerging of Eden under water now known as the northern part of the Persian Gulf.

The first major change to the earth occurred earlier following the expulsion of Adam and Eve from the garden. In Eden there were no thorns and thistles.[76] Adam in the days following his expulsion began to see all kinds of weeds and poisonous plants.

There were changes in the animal kingdom. Eve had conversed with the serpent. Now poisonous vipers appeared whose bite could kill you. Adam, I think, communicated with lions. After Eden, lions would attack humans and tear them apart. The nature of animals changed; some remained herbivorous while others became carnivorous. The nature of humankind had changed, which we will note when we reference Cain, the first son of Adam. The world became a dangerous place to live.

---

76   Part of the punishment for Adam's sin was the cursing of the ground of planet earth. Prior to Adam's sin, there were no thorns or thistles. After Adam's sin, there were earth changes. We don't know how extent they were. Read Genesis 3:17–19. Earth changes of course have continued like in the day of Cain.

Whether animals quit their bodies prior to Adam's disobedience is not clear. There is a sense in which animals do not die.[77] Animals are not moral creatures. They are not held by God to the standard He has set for humans. They have never been separated from God. But with the entrance of death on planet earth, animals suffer because of the penalty of separation brought by Adam's disobedience. As humans expire because of ill health, disease, extermination, or the aging process, so the animal kingdom and all of creation are afflicted. The apostle Paul reveals that the whole creation is under the bondage of corruption. It will be delivered when the Son of God, Jesus, comes back in His second coming and Christians, the sons and daughters of God, come in resurrected, glorified bodies, bringing the creation redemption—freedom from the Devil, death, and sin. Paul wrote,

> For I consider that the sufferings of this present time are not worthy to be compared with the glory which shall be revealed to us. For the earnest expectation of the creation eagerly waits for the revealing of the sons of God. For the creation was subjected to futility not willingly, but because of Him who subjected it in hope: because the creation itself also will be delivered from the bondage of corruption into the glorious liberty of the children of God. For we know that the whole creation groans and labors with birth pangs until now. Not only that, but we also who have the first fruits of the Spirit, even we ourselves groan within ourselves, eagerly waiting for the adoption, the redemption of our bodies. (Rom. 8:18–23)

Isaiah, the prophet, wrote about the time of which Paul prophesied when Eden-like conditions will be restored.

---

77 Biblical death is separation from God. On the day Adam disobeyed God and ate of the forbidden fruit, he died. While animals physically die, they probably do not die in the way that humans in the image of God die.

The wolf also shall dwell with the lamb, the leopard shall lie down with the young goat, the calf and the young lion and the fatling together; and a little child shall lead them. The cow and the bear shall graze; their young ones shall lie down together; and the lion shall eat straw like the ox. The nursing child shall play by the cobra's hole, and the weaned child shall put his hand in the viper's den. They shall not hurt nor destroy in all My holy mountain, For the earth shall be full of the knowledge of the Lord As the waters cover the sea. (Isa. 11:6–9)

26

Sexuality

Adam and Eve, as husband and wife, had sexual relations. We read, "Now Adam knew his wife, and she conceived and bore Cain, and said, 'I have acquired a man from the Lord.' Then she bore again, this time his brother Abel" (Gen. 4:1–2).

Genesis 5:4 informs us Adam had sons and daughters. Since Adam was told, "Be fruitful and fill the earth," he had many children (Gen.1:28).

Adam and Eve were to have children. The sex act in marriage is therefore commanded by God thus sanctified or made holy. Sex between a husband and a wife is good.

Biblically, when a man knows a woman, it means he has sex with her. Sex for bearing children is not the only reason a husband and wife are to have intercourse. The apostle Paul wrote, "It is better to marry than to burn with passion" (1 Cor. 7:9 NIV). Paul knew human beings have a natural drive to fulfill sexual needs, so he taught that it is God's will for a man and a woman to get married to fulfill their sexual drive honorably in the estate of matrimony. That's why he wrote, "Because of sexual immorality, let each man have his own wife, and let each woman have her own husband" (1 Cor. 7:2). In verse 3 he instructed each man to render the proper affection toward his wife, and the wife was to do the same toward her husband. In verse 4, he continues that the husband, for the purpose of sex, has authority over his wife's body, and the wife has authority over the husband's body. In verse 5 he taught they were not to deprive each other. Since the beginning, with Adam and Eve, a husband and a wife, has had the need for sexual intercourse.

Our Creator built into us a drive to have sex. Our sex drive is necessary for us to have children, yet not everyone can have children. Note Eve said, "I have acquired a man from the Lord" (Gen. 4:1). Sexuality for Adam and Eve or for a husband and a wife is twofold.

First, sexual intercourse is part of the marital relationship. It bonds a man and a woman, a husband and a wife, together in a healthy way. It is part of a loving relationship and may be called love making, "the act of marriage." Tim LaHaye and his wife, Beverly, in their book *The Act of Marriage* teach that God designed our sex organs for pleasure. Sex, as the Bible teaches in 1 Corinthians 7, is for a married couple's enjoyment.[78] It's not only for having children.

Second, sexual intercourse in marriage is also for having children. As already noted, there are those in marriage who have sexual intercourse without having children. Many married couples, due to physical complications, cannot have children.

It is also true that sexual intercourse is not necessary in a marriage. Here it is acknowledged that some, due to physical complications through birth, an illness, or some mishap, are not capable of having sex. Such relationships, built around spiritual principles, vocational or social interests, personal fulfillment, or other factors, can be happy ones.

Adam and Eve probably had sexual intercourse before being expelled from Eden. The LaHayes believe Adam and Eve did have sex before sin

---

78   Tim and Beverly LaHaye, *The Act of Marriage*. (Grand Rapids, MI: Zondervan Publishing House, 1976), 36–37.

entered the picture.[79] Since Eve said, "I have acquired a man from the Lord" (Gen. 4:1), it is possible that Adam and Eve had had sex many times but up until her statement she had never gotten pregnant and received a man from the Lord.

---

79 Ibid., 36.

27

Family

Adam and Eve were a family. A family by biblical standards, our resource teaches, has a husband and a wife. A biblical family, however, involves more; it is tripartite. Through the study of Adam in the book of Genesis we learn:

1. The history of the family begins with Adam.

2. God started the family. It is of divine origin.

3. God created Adam first. In the beginning God was, and then Adam. Get the point. It was God and Adam. God modeled with Adam to illustrate the relationship every person is to have prior to relationship with one's spouse.

4. Today a woman, like her counterpart, the man, is to have a relationship with God before getting married.

5. When a man and woman get married and leave their family of origin, each should already be in relationship with his or her Creator. God is our primary relationship before marriage and following marriage.

After the death of the departed loved one, it is once again God, the Creator, and the remaining spouse. God is vertically our priority relationship, and our spouse is horizontally our primary earthly relationship. The family relationship is threefold, tripartite. Recognizing Adam's creation and what it entails means a marriage or family is to include three persons— God the Creator, a husband, and a wife.

Second, a family may have children—one, two, or many. God intended families to have children. A husband and a wife, however, do not have to have children to be a family. In earth's history, at least in the past, most families have had children.

Adam and Eve were the first family, and as such they had many children. God created Adam and Eve for Himself and for each other, and God gave them children.

28

Children

The first three sons of Adam were Cain, Abel (Gen. 4:1–2), and Seth (Gen. 4:25–26). Adam probably had many more. These three are named because they were the first three men born on earth in the first family. Each of them has special significance. Adam and Eve also had daughters—evidently many of them (Gen. 5:4).

It is of tremendous importance to know that mankind was created. We are descended from Adam. Our history on this subject is valid. In addition, God gave us the family. His divine intention is for us to live in families. Part of this whole arrangement has to do with children. Children come from God. Our resource teaches.

> Children are a gift from God; they are his reward. Children born to a young man are like sharp arrows to defend him. Happy is the man who has his quiver full of them. That man shall have the help he needs when arguing with his enemies. (Ps. 127:3–5 TLB)

That children are from God, according to the purpose of God, is a truth emphasized throughout our resource. Eve acknowledged that her sons were given to her by God. Abraham, the chosen one through whose family God would fulfill Genesis 3:15, was promised a son. Though he had sexual intercourse with his wife Sarah again and again, Sarah was not given a son until twenty-five years after God's promise. In Sarah's old age, she became pregnant and had a son, Isaac, a miracle baby. Isaac was a gift from God.[80]

This truth that children come from God is also taught through the experiences of Hannah, who bore Samuel (1 Sam. 1:1–27), Elizabeth, who bore John the Baptist (Luke 1:5–25, 57–80), and even Mary, who bore Jesus, the Savior (Luke 1:26–38, 2:1–7). We understand Moses, Samson, and Jeremiah were all special gifts from God. In fact, every single baby is a gift from God. Children are sacred. A child is not a blob of flesh that can be cut out of a human being and thrown away as garbage because it is unwanted.

The Christian viewpoint is that a woman's body does not belong to her but to the Creator. The apostle Paul wrote to Christians, "Do you not know that your body is a temple of the Holy Spirit, who is in you, whom you have received from God? You are not your own" (1 Cor. 6:19 NIV).

Concerning children, you may also have observed that the daughters of Adam were not named. Neither were all the sons of Adam. Three were named. We will address the reasons in following chapters. Women, however, are no less important than men.

Shortly after I became a chaplain in the US Air Force in Biloxi, Mississippi, I met the second woman chaplain in the history of that branch of service. She greatly impressed me. Actually, I thought she was a better speaker than most of the other fifteen chaplains on base. When assigned a worship service jointly with another chaplain, the chaplain would not work with her. In short, he did not see a woman as qualified to preach. She contributed to my ministry positively.

---

80 Sarah was ninety years old, past the age of having children, when she birthed Isaac (Gen. 17:1–17, 18:1–14, 21:1–3).

The first woman in the Bible, Eve, is mentioned by name. She was Adam's equal, comparable to him (Gen. 2:20). Sarah was a woman of great stature in that she honored her husband, Abraham, obeying him (1 Peter 3:6). She sought to avoid the folly of Eve, who did not obey Adam's instruction regarding the Tree of the Knowledge of Good and Evil. Rebekah, Isaac's wife, knew more about God's will for their children than Isaac did (Gen. 25:20–23).

Deborah, a prophetess in the days of the Judges, was a woman of such power with God that Barak, a Hebrew military leader, would not go to war against Israel's enemies, the Canaanites, without her. Her song of victory, which gives a woman authorship in the Bible, is in Judges 5. Ruth, a Moabite woman who would not leave her suffering mother-in-law, a Hebrew, was one of the finest human beings who ever lived. The great-grandmother of King David, she has a book in the Bible named after her. It contains one of the most beautiful stories in the Bible, one as inspiring as can be found in history.

Huldah, a prophetess, spokeswoman for God, was sought out by Hilkiah, the high priest of Israel, and others to hear the word of the Lord in the days of King Josiah (2 Kings 22:14–20). In the days of the New Testament, Philip, an evangelist, had four daughters who prophesied or spoke for the Lord (Acts 21:1–9).

Anna, a prophetess who was well known in Jerusalem at the time of Jesus' birth, immediately recognized baby Jesus for who He was, giving testimony to Him proclaiming redemption for Jerusalem (Luke 2:36–38). Much more can be acknowledged on the importance of women, the daughters in our families. Mary, a holy woman, had the privilege of fulfilling Genesis 3:15 and birthing the Son of God to save planet earth.

That a woman would be ruled by a man (Gen. 3:16) was part of the curse brought upon Eve and all women as a result of the fall. With the advent of Jesus Christ and the triumph of His gospel, through the forgiveness of our sin, that curse is removed. A Christian man and a Christian woman should not be part of a malaise in which the woman is trying to control her husband and the man is seeking to rule his wife. The husband is a Christ figure (Eph. 5:23–33), and the wife is a Holy Spirit figure—a helper (comparable to a man, Gen. 3:20), *paraclete* in the Greek. She is one who stands beside (John 14:15–18, 25–26, 15:26, 16:7–15). The Christian relationship for a man and woman, a husband and wife, in a family, a tripartite relationship, is Trinitarian. Jesus Christ vertically represents God, the husband horizontally, represents Christ, and the wife horizontally represents the Holy Spirit. The Trinity, with perfect unity, is our model for the family. Like children, sons and daughters born of the Holy Spirit through Jesus Christ, sons and daughters are given to humankind through our Creator, Jesus.

Sons and daughters, our children, we recognize are gifts of infinite value. They grow into men and women, having enormous potential. The stories of honorable men and women in mankind's history are inspirational, remarkable, and a tribute to our Creator. They are our stories—yours and mine.

29

Cain and Abel

Adam and Eve raised their first two children, sons, Cain and Abel, outside Eden. It seems Abel had the prominence, for he is mentioned first in Genesis 4:2. Abel was a keeper of sheep. That is to say, he began to gather sheep. Evidently he raised sheep, using their wool to clothe Adam and Eve and their family.

Cain, mentioned second in Genesis 4:2, was a tiller of the ground, a gardener like his father, Adam. The Scripture doesn't say what Cain raised. He must have grown a number of crops.

Genesis 4:3 (NIV) states, "In the course of time" which means the boys aged and became men. While we don't know much about them, we are informed about an important occurrence in their lives. They both worshipped God, Cain making an offering of fruit from the ground and Abel making an offering to God from his flock. God, the Lord or the Son of God, respected Abel's offering, but He did not respect Cain's.

Surely Abel was pleased, but it's Cain who is mentioned. Cain was angry, and his countenance fell. His physical expression was soured, embittered toward his brother, Abel, assuredly God, and others (Gen. 4:5). The Living Bible Translation puts it this way: "His face grew dark with fury."

The Lord, as is His practice, addressed the issue. He spoke to Cain, saying, "Why are you angry? Why is your face downcast?" (Gen. 4:6 NIV). The LBT has, "Why is your face so dark with rage?" Then the Lord, as is His way, gave His word, "If you do what is right, will you not be accepted?" (Gen. 4:7 NIV). In other words, something Cain did not do, a wrong action, evidently based on a wrong attitude, is why God didn't approve Cain's offering. God, as always, is just. The way to approval was simple. Do the right thing with the right attitude, and all will be well. Such is God's standard for acceptance or righteousness. All could have been well with Cain. It was up to him. Cain had the ability by the prerogative of choice to make everything okay.

God went further in giving Cain insight into his problem. He said to Cain, "And if you do not do what is right, sin is crouching at your door. It desires to have you, but you must master it" (Gen. 4:7 NIV). The Living Bible has, "Sin is waiting to attack you, longing to destroy you. But you can conquer it."

Cain, however, did not conquer sin. "It came to pass when they [Cain and Abel] were in the field, that Cain rose up against Abel his brother and killed him" (Gen. 4:8). Adding to all the difficulties that entered the relationship of Adam and Eve following their eating of the forbidden fruit, now one son killed the other son; the firstborn killed the second born. Our resource presents us with the truth, the life of the first family as it was.

Though Adam and Eve's sin separated them from God, the Lord, the Son of God, continued to providentially care for them. God asked Cain, "Where is your brother Abel?" (Gen. 4:9 NIV). It's interesting that God knows us by name. He refers to our names when He addresses us. He cares!

God, of course, knew where Abel was! He had the same kind of conversation with Adam when Adam sinned. Cain was not a nice person. Replying to God—Almighty God—he snidely uttered, "I do not know.

Am I my brother's keeper?" (Gen. 4:9). The truth was that Cain did know. In his caustic remark, his feelings about Abel were apparent. He did not care about his brother Abel. Cain made it clear that what happened to Abel was of no concern to him. The fact that Abel was his brother meant nothing. Have no doubt about it—God's principles for a family and for mankind have always been the same. The Son of God would later teach that we are to love God with all our heart, soul, mind, and strength and that we are to love others as our self (Mark 12:30–31). Cain was to love his brother. However, he did not love Abel. Cain hated his brother, so he killed him.

Obviously God wants us to care about others, our brothers. God created Adam and Eve, and through them He is the Maker of every human being on planet earth. Again and again in our resource God contextually reminds us that He is our Maker. We were put on this planet to care for it and for each other. The power of love is the strongest force in our world. The power of hate, the second-strongest force on planet earth, divides us into factions that seek to kill, destroy, and hurt the other. Again, our resource gives us insight. As it was in the beginning, so it is right now. Again and again, the Bible tells it like it is!

30

Sin

God said to Cain, "Sin is crouching at your door" (Gen. 4:7 NIV). This is the first time the word *sin* is used in the Bible. God spoke of sin as a reality—something that exists. Sin is the evil, from Satan, that is in us working against God to destroy His creation and every human being, individually and corporately.

When Adam disobeyed God by eating of the fruit on the Tree of the Knowledge of Good and Evil, Adam sinned. Adam opened his mind to the suggestions of Satan. When Adam followed Satan rather than God, sin, as the power of Satan, entered his heart, the seat of his emotions and affections.

Sin is a disease not in the sense of sickness caused by bacteria but an illness of the spirit that destroys one's soul. Like smallpox, sin spread from Adam to the whole human race. God put planet earth into quarantine to protect the rest of what is out there from us. The cure for our condition, a spiritual one, is redemption through Jesus Christ, the Son of God.

The Greek word for sin in the New Testament is *hamartia*, a falling away or missing the right path.[81] God's standard for acceptance is called

---

81 Merrill F. Unger, *Unger's Bible Dictionary*. (Chicago: Moody Press, 1970), 1028.

righteousness. To be righteous is to be without sin. But no one is without sin. "There is none who does good"—that is who is without fault. No one is right according to God's standard (Ps. 14:1). "All have sinned and fall short of the glory of God" (Rom. 3:23 NIV).

In the New Testament there are four statements that give insight about sin. The apostle John tells us "sin is lawlessness" (1 John 3:4 NIV). To sin is to break the commands of God. In particular note Exodus 20:1–17. Actually the whole of the Law given to Israel illustrates sinfulness. The Law prophetically points to our need of Jesus Christ. That's why the apostle Paul wrote, "The law was our tutor to bring us to Christ" (Gal. 3:24).

Second, "all unrighteousness is sin" (1 John 5:17). Unrighteousness is missing the mark. In Galatians the apostle Paul lists the fruit the Holy Spirit produces in a born-again person's spirit—love, joy, peace, longsuffering, kindness, goodness, faithfulness, gentleness, and self-control (Gal. 5:19–23). Sin, on the other hand, or the Satanic works of the flesh are adultery, fornication, uncleanness, lewdness, idolatry, sorcery, hatred, contentions, jealousies, outbursts of wrath, selfish ambitions, dissensions, heresies, envy, murders, drunkenness, revelries, and the like.

Third, James, the brother of Jesus, taught "Anyone, then, who knows the good he ought to do and doesn't do it, sins" (James 4:17 NIV). This is called the sin of omission. James clearly teaches when we are not our brother's keeper, we sin. We are responsible to help others.

Fourth, the apostle Paul also taught, "Whatever is not from faith is sin" (Rom. 14:23). Adam was told not to eat fruit from the Tree of the Knowledge of Good and Evil. If he did eat, he would die. Adam, by taking God at His word, was to demonstrate faith in Him. God requires faith as the means to get right with Him. The writer of the book of Hebrews teaches us, "Without faith it is impossible to please God, because anyone who comes to him must believe that he exists and that he rewards those who earnestly seek him " (Heb. 11:6 NIV).

Cain did not believe what God told him. Sin was about to possess him. Cain's hatred for his brother festered in him like water that became hotter and hotter until it boiled over into the physical act of murder. Cain did not have to murder his brother. If he had changed his thinking, as God advised him to do, he would not have killed his brother.

Jesus, the Son of God, gives us insight into our spiritual condition. Our speech betrays where we are in regard to sin.

> Those things which proceed out of the mouth come from the heart and they defile a man. For out of the heart proceed evil thoughts, murders, adulteries, fornications, thefts, false witness, and blasphemies. These are the things which defile. (Matt. 15:18–20)

Note that Jesus teaching on the condition that defiles a person—that which leads us to acting out sinful behavior against God—begins with evil thoughts. These thoughts come from within a person—from the seat of one's emotions and affections. They identify who one is.

Personalizing it, when sin lays at my door, the proper response is to repent of my sin and seek forgiveness through Jesus Christ. New life in Jesus Christ renews my mind and my thought processes, and that renewal results in a positive transformation in the person I am (Rom. 12:1–2).

31

Murder

Adam's son Cain killed his son Abel. Put another way, the first human born on planet earth became a murderer. Murder among humankind existed from the beginning. The firstborn human killed the second-born human. Death had not been occurring over millennia and millennia, nor was it a natural thing that regularly happened; it was not something to which humankind had to adjust. The first death of a human on planet earth was a killing. It was murder.

When Cain killed Abel, it had nothing to do with the survival of the fittest. The fittest did not survive. Cain committed a definite premeditated act called murder, in which he took his brother's life. It is forbidden by God. The sixth commandment is, "You shall not murder" (Ex. 20:13 NIV). Before it was written in the Bible in the Old Testament Law God gave to Israel at Mount Sinai, God put into humankind's innermost being or conscience that you must not kill another human being. All humans know it is wrong to kill another human being.

When Cain killed his brother Abel, Cain took the most precious thing Abel had—his life. Cain's killing was an act of the will. He was accountable for what he did. Since God gives life, no one is to take it away—except God.

Under our chapter on sin, murder is recognized as sin. Murder is a result of sin. When Cain killed Abel, Adam and Eve were shocked. Here was a happening that affected Adam and his wife deeply, emotionally, one that was a direct result of their disobedience to God. In Abel's demise, Adam and Eve experienced a horrendous aftereffect of their separation from God.

It was not characteristic of Adam to kill. Beginning with Cain, we have a long history of humankind wanting to kill. One of the reasons God destroyed mankind in the days of Noah was because the earth was filled with violence (Gen. 6:11). We don't know how Cain slew Abel. Some have pictured Cain hitting Abel in the head with a rock. Perhaps in his fury Cain hit Abel again and again. It was a brutal scene. Murder is a reality of sin!

Cain used violence against Abel. Five generations later, Cain's descendant Lamech would follow his example and kill a man (Gen. 4:16–24). Others would kill.

Communities would learn to make weapons and attack other communities to satisfy their lust for things and women. James the brother of Jesus tells us wars and fights come from internal compulsion inside us (James 4:1). War became glorified. Nations became proud of their ability to kill others and take their land, resources, or whatever it might be. John the Baptist taught "do violence to no man" (Luke 3:14 KJV).

To kill something is to destroy it. History records humans like to kill things. The word *Satan* means "adversary" or "opponent."[82] Satan, who sets us against each other, is a destroyer. Jesus called the Devil (Satan) "a murderer from the beginning" (John 8:44 NIV). It was Satan who entered the mind of Cain, giving him murderous thoughts. Cain, who opened his mind to the Devil and sin, allowed himself to be overpowered with murderous images in his mind. Cain imagined

---

82   Ibid., 972–3.

killing his brother, Abel, over and over until he actually committed the murderous act.

I personally have seen how this process works. I have a nephew who was incarcerated because of mental problems. While visiting with him, he told me he had given himself to Satan. I warned him there would be serious consequences. Sometime later, during a weekend release, he shot and killed my father and seriously wounded his own father, who later died. He claimed the Devil led him to do it. Most psychologists think such ideas about a devil or the Devil are a result of delusional thinking.

Jesus knew the religious leaders of Jerusalem were planning to kill Him. The apostle John informs us concerning Jesus, "He was in the world, and though the world was made through Him, the world did not recognize Him" (John 1:10 NIV). Jesus said to those leaders,

> You seek to kill Me, a Man Who has told you the truth … You do the deeds of your father … You are of your father the devil, and the desires of your father you want to do. He was a murderer from the beginning. (John 8:40–44)

God said to Cain, "What have you done?" (Gen. 4:10 NIV). Actually Cain probably didn't really understand what he had done, but Cain was guilty of murder. God said to Cain, "The voice of your brother's blood cries out to Me from the ground" (Gen. 4:10). A person may kill another person, but that is not the end. Abel's body ceased to function, but Abel's spirit continued to live. Abel cried out to God for justice. Abel's blood had spilled into the earth, the ground made for man's life. The ground was defiled. It had to be purified. Someone would have to cleanse it to pay for Cain's trespass. God said to Cain,

> So now you are cursed from the earth which has opened its mouth to receive your brother's blood from your hand. When you till the ground, it shall no longer yield

its strength to you. A fugitive and a Vagabond you shall
be on the earth. (Gen. 4:11–12)

Originally Adam, because of his sin, was told the earth would now yield
thorns and thistles (Gen. 3:18). Now more change occurred. Life would
be harder. Cain and his descendants would have to move from place to
place due to horticultural and climatic conditions.

There are consequences because of our sin. Our resource tells us, "There
is a generation that is pure in its own eyes, Yet is not washed from its
filthiness" (Prov. 30:12). Does man think he can kill millions of babies
and not defile his land? Does he think he can take life given by God
without consequences? As someone has said, "The wheel of God's justice
grinds very slowly, but when it grinds, it grinds very fine."

Thus says the Lord, "Do not defile the land where you live" (Num. 35:34
NIV). "Do not pollute the land where you are. Bloodshed pollutes the
land, and atonement cannot be made for the Land on which the blood has
been shed, except by the blood of the one who shed it" (Num. 35:33 NIV).
Woe! Woe! Woe!

32

Capital Punishment

Adam knew something about capital punishment. It was the price Jesus, the Son of God, would pay to take away the sin of Adam and Eve, as well as that of all those who would be redeemed. Jesus would pay with His blood to take away the sin of repentant murderers. More will be written in regard to this subject.

Capital punishment, which is prescribed by God for the sin of murder, is commanded in our resource. Some have called the period from Noah to the giving of the Law the Starlight Period, the period from the Law to the beginning of Christ's church as the Moonlight Period, and the period of the church of Christ as the Sunlight Period. Capital punishment was established by God in all three of these periods. It was not commanded during mankind's first period, from Adam to Noah.[83]

---

83 1. The four periods of biblical history up to and including our present epoch are:
   Period Number One: From Adam in the creation to Noah through the great flood (Gen. 1–8).
   Period Number Two: From the covenant God made with Noah to the giving of the Law, the covenant God made with Israel at Mount Sinai (Gen. 9–50, Ex. 1–18).
   Period Number Three: From the Law received by Israel in Exodus 19–40, Leviticus, Numbers, and Deuteronomy through the Old Testament period in the books Joshua through Malachi through the time of Jesus in the gospels of the New

When God told Cain some of the consequences of his sin, Cain said, "My punishment is more than I can bear" (Gen. 4:13 NIV). It doesn't appear that Cain owned up to what he had done. No repentance was evident.[84]

Cain said, "Anyone who finds me shall kill me" (Gen. 4:14). He understood that by taking his brother's life he had forfeited his own. Cain knew he no longer deserved to live. He was an intelligent being. He understood justice.

The Lord answered, "If anyone kills Cain, he will suffer vengeance seven times over" (Gen. 4:15 NIV). There is no escaping the justice of God. God knows everything we do and everything we think. There will be a reckoning, a judgment (Acts 24:24–25). No one is going to get away with anything. "Vengeance is Mine, I will repay" says the Lord (Rom. 12:19). In the day of Adam, however, no one was to kill Cain.

In Noah's era, post-flood, things changed. God said,

Testament, Matthew, Mark, Luke, and John to the beginning of the church in the book of Acts 2.

Period Number Four: From the beginning of the church through the New Testament time until the Second Coming of Jesus Christ in the New Testament from Acts 2 through Revelation. Capital punishment was commanded by God in the periods two through four.

84   Cain's remark, "My punishment is greater than I can bear" (Gen. 4:13) indicates he was not going to bear his punishment. That is, Cain did not accept God's verdict. He would no longer seek God's favor. Cain would build his own kingdom and work for a world according to his making rather than God's. Therefore Augustine rightly attributes to Cain the founding of the Earthly City as over and against the City of God. "Thus the founder of the earthly city was a fratricide. Overcome with envy, he slew his own brother, a citizen of the eternal city, and a sojourner on earth. So that we cannot be surprised that this first specimen, or, as the Greeks say, archetype of crime, should, long afterwards, find a corresponding crime at his foundation of that city which was destined to reign over many nations, and be the head of this earthly city of which we speak. For of that city, also, as one of their poets has mentioned, 'the first walls were stained with a brother's blood,' of as Roman history records, Remus was slain by his brother Romulus." Augustine, translated by Rev. Marcus Dods, *The Nicene and Post Nicene Fathers, Volume II, The City of God.* (Grand Rapids, MI: Zondervan, 1979), 286.

Surely for your lifeblood I will demand a reckoning;
from the hand of every beast I will require it, and from
the hand of man. From the hand of every man's brother I
will require the life of man. Whoever sheds man's blood,
By man his blood shall be shed; For in the image of God
He made man. (Gen. 9:5–6)

It is clear here that God established the penalty of capital punishment for killing a human being—that is, for murder.

An animal that killed a human was to be killed. Such was specified in the Law Moses received on Mount Sinai. Read Exodus 21:28–29.

When a person murdered another person, his or her life was to be taken. The reason the murder of a human being is so terrible is because a man or woman is made in the image of God. A human is not an evolved animal, a specialized ape. To kill a human being is a direct attack against the Creator. It is to remove from the planet a being created for heaven, eternity, and glory.

To terminate such a life is so serious that it requires the life of the person who does so. Every human being on planet earth is to live a life in which he or she has opportunity to establish a right relationship with God and to develop under His direction the life to be lived in eternity. Cain could not understand in his earthly setting what he did by terminating Abel. No matter how intelligent a person may think he or she is, it is impossible in our present setting to totally comprehend what we have done to another when that person is murdered. This is true with each baby that is aborted.

In a justice system, a person who murders another often has opportunity that the person murdered does not. A murderer, who has to pay the price for his or her crime, has the time to repent and be forgiven—that is get right with God and go to heaven. Jesus, the Son of God, said, "Do not be afraid of those who kill the body but cannot kill the soul. Rather, be afraid of the One who can destroy both soul and body in hell" (Matt. 10:28 NIV).

Capital punishment was not instituted by God as a deterrent to prevent murder. It was command for the purpose of justice. It did not begin for those who are Jews and Christians under the Old Testament Law. It began as part of the covenant God made with Noah that encompasses all humankind on planet earth (Gen. 9:1–17). As such it is to be part of a governmental system where it is administered equally though proper jurisprudence. Such a system has no right to forgive an individual when that person commits murder. Mercy belongs to God and God alone. To be forgiven by God does not mean the penalty—forfeiture of one's life—no longer applies. It is the duty of a proper court of law to administer appropriate justice. Justice for a convicted premeditated murder is capital punishment.

Capital punishment was commanded by the Law.[85] Moses, receiving instruction from God, wrote, "Anyone who strikes a man and kills him shall surely be put to death" (Ex. 21:12 NIV). To be sure, the Law made distinctions about the penalty for killing another according to the way the killing was done. There were provisions for a person's protection if that person had not premeditated killing. For the person guilty of premeditated murder, there was no leniency. "If a man acts with premeditation against his neighbor, to kill him by treachery, you may take him from My altar [a place of protection] that he may die" (Ex. 21:14). To get some idea on these things, read Exodus 21:12–27.

Some thoughts: Moses killed an Egyptian, and he himself was not killed. He did have to flee Egypt and lived in the wilderness for forty years. David gave a command he knew would eventuate in one of his men being killed. God punished him but not with capital punishment. The apostle Paul was probably responsible for the death of the first Christian martyr, Stephen, but God, by His grace, forgave Paul.

---

85   *The Law* refers to the covenant Moses received for Israel at Mount Sinai.

The Apostle Paul's writing in Romans 13 gives us New Testament follow-on to the teaching of capital punishment in the Old Testament Law. Paul instructs Christians to be subject to governmental authorities. Paul wrote, concerning the power of our governor,

> He is God's minister to you for good. But if you do evil, be afraid; for he does not bear the sword in vain; for he is God's minister an avenger to execute wrath on him who practices evil. (Rom. 13:4)

It's quite possible that God did not have Cain executed because there was no earthly government at that time. Adam would have had to carry out the sentence. God would not ask Adam to kill his own son. God also gives us the freedom to see what it's like when He is not in our lives. When we live without God, we live in hate, vengeance, and violence.

God clearly teaches us what we are not to do. Even though Cain knew it was wrong to kill his brother, he had never received a commandment not to do so. That may be another reason why God did not take his life. Although God could have punished Cain immediately, He did not. God does not always punish us for our iniquities right away. He is merciful and gracious. He knows we are dust (Ps. 103:8–14). But justice must be done, and justice will be done. Every person will be judged for his or her sin.

Cain's descendant, Lamech, killed a man. He was aware that Cain was not punished. So Lamech said, "If Cain is avenged seven times [if someone kills him for killing Abel], then Lamech seventy-seven times" (Gen. 4:24 NIV). God did not say seventy-sevenfold. Lamech said it. The context of Genesis 4, tracing Cain's descendants to Lamech, has to do with an epilogue on Cain's murder and its aftereffects. Lamech took God's mercy toward Cain as a license to murder. Violence spread until people were murdering others everywhere.

33

Father

Adam was a father. He had no precedent modeling fatherhood. There were no seminars on parenting. Evidently much of his time involved learning how to adjust to his new circumstance. Before the advent of our modern era, much of a family's time was spent doing what one had to do to live.

Cain and Abel had no computers, musical instruments, radio, or television. Doubtless, Adam did not take his boys fishing or hunting. There were no sports or scout programs. They probably never flew a kite, played marbles, or made models of man's inventions. What did Adam do with his sons as a father?

Surely Adam taught his sons about animals. They may have had numerous pets. Naturally, Adam taught his sons horticulture, shepherding, and farming. Adam, the intelligent person that he was, taught his sons skills he acquired relating to their new environment.

Certainly the children's knowledge included how to prepare vegetables and fruit for healthy consumption. Adam and his sons were not nut and berry gatherers. Necessity meant learning how to construct shelter, evidently from wood or stones, make clothes, and take care of self and others. Eve, of course, was part of all that transpired. Adam modeled for the boys, and evidently for their female children, a good relationship between a husband and a wife.

Adam, Eve, and their boys and girls spent their time together. All activities were family activities. Adam told his sons how he was created and Eve was made. Adam told his children about God, Eden, trees in its midst, God's command, their fall, God's promise, and His provision. Evidently they studied the heavens, the constellations, time, and the making of a calendar, other creatures, and the person of God Himself.

Inquisitiveness led Adam on hikes with his sons and daughters, engaging in exploration. Actually, there was much to do, for planet earth was a wonderful place to live. One would never tire of learning what creation is about, how to understand and use it. Some of these particulars have to do with what is called science. Science does not mean we no longer need God. Science has to do with learning how to use what God has given us in His Creation. It teaches us to appreciate God.

Adam was up to the task of inventing whatever he needed to be happy and do well. He and his posterity learned how to use creation for man's felicity. Later King Solomon of Israel would write, philosophizing about contemporary life, "There is nothing new under the sun" (Eccl. 1:9 NIV). "Is there anything of which one can say, 'Look! This is something new'? It was here long ago. It was here before our time" (Eccl. 1:10 NIV).

Solomon went on to write,

> I have seen the God-given task with which the sons of men are to be occupied. He has made everything beautiful in its time. Also He has put eternity in their hearts, except that no one can find out the work that God does from beginning to end. I know that nothing is better for them than to rejoice and to do good in their lives, and also that every man should eat and drink and enjoy the good of all his labor—it is the gift of God. (Eccl. 3:10–13)

Certainly Solomon's observation, insight, and revelation began in Adam.

There is every reason to think Adam was a most wonderful father. Here it is significant to understand that a person can be a good father and still have a child who becomes a criminal or a detestable son or daughter.

It is true that Adam himself messed up. It was no fault of his Father, our heavenly Father the Creator Himself. God was benevolent. His love was expressed to Adam in every possible way. God's parental care was perfect. God created His son Adam as a free moral agent who was accountable for his actions. Adam made a wrong choice. The failure was Adam's, not God's.

The same was true with Cain. Yes, Adam's choice to eat of the fruit on the Tree of the Knowledge of Good and Evil brought sin to planet earth. And it was Cain's choice to kill his brother Abel. Cain's behavior was not due to faulty parenthood. Cain's action had to do with evil in him, a choice to listen to Satan rather than God. He was not only unrighteous in what he thought, but he condemned himself by what he did.

God makes it clear in His teaching that every person is responsible for his or her own sin. Moses wrote in the Law, "Fathers shall not be put to death for their children, nor children put to death for their fathers; each is to die for their own sin" (Deut. 24:16 NIV).

Adam was the father of Cain, but he was also the father of Abel, of whom we have good things to say. It is true that a good home environment and good parenting are highly contributory to how our children fare in life. But the decisions made by a child, good or bad, are to that child's credit or dishonor. A parent who has a child who makes evil choices may have influenced that child in that way. Then again, that child's parents may not have had anything to do with the wrong choice or choices that child makes. Today there are many influences other than one's parents. It has always been so. To be sure, there is always, and always has been, Satan and his influence. Because a child turns out to be a murderer is not necessarily the fault of his or her parent or parents. Knowing this should cause fathers and mothers not to torture themselves with guilt over a bad apple—a Cain or a Cainette.

34

Death

Adam experienced death. The meaning of death is separation from God. On the day Adam ate of the forbidden fruit, he died. He no longer walked with the Creator in the cool of the garden. He no longer felt the gentle breeze of the Holy Spirit. He spoke to God, and God heard him. God answered benevolently but no longer with an audible voice. Adam had walked with God personally—that is, there had been light, a radiant aura, and a physical voice. Now man must walk with God by faith. The way out of death—life—would be through faith in the Son of God.

Adam and Eve further felt the pain of death through the loss of Abel, their second son. They missed Abel, his smile, his voice, his presence, and his delight in his animals, especially his sheep. They could remember eating with Abel, happy times, times of laughter and fun. Eve could remember Abel's first moments, how she suckled him at her breast. They could remember his first steps. Adam and Eve still had a few toys with which he loved to play. There were his clothes and the instruments with which he had worked with the sheep. Adam and Eve could see where he had slept. Now Abel was gone.

They didn't know where he lay. There was no closure for them. They thought and thought about what they could do. It became evident that there was nothing they could do. There was no answer for death. Only

God could help. The problem of death is not one man can solve. Nothing has changed in human history. Adam's biggest problem and ours too is we are all headed to the same end. King David called it "the way of all the earth" (1 Kings 2:2 NIV). Everyone must physically die. Of course, Abel did not go the way of the earth or die a natural death. Abel died a physical death according to the way of Cain. There is that too, much of it on planet earth.

Certain Christian pastors tell us at memorial services that death is our friend. They have in mind that death is the end of our earthly sojourn and now Christians cross the great divide between us and heaven to be in the presence of God. However, that's not what my Bible teaches about death. The apostle Paul wrote, "The last enemy that will be destroyed is death" (1 Cor. 15:26). Death is not our friend. Death is an enemy. There is nothing good about death. Death stinks!

The apostle Paul teaches us that death comes because of our sin. "The wages of sin is death" (Rom. 6:23 NIV). The good news is that Jesus Christ the promised one of Genesis 3:15 came to destroy death. He came to destroy the work of Satan and his instrument, death. Jesus came as Eve's "Seed" (Gen. 3:15) that through His death, "He might destroy him who holds the power of death - that is, the devil" (Heb. 2:14).

Our resource on this subject is progressive. But surely Adam understood that though Abel had died, he would see him again. The Lord, the Son of God, had begun to teach Adam and Eve on this subject with Genesis 3:15 and the animal skins God gave them for clothes. The way of sin is death, but the free gift of God is eternal life.

Being expelled from Eden, Adam and Eve suffered great loss. Now that Abel had been born, raised, and murdered, things seemed even worse. Death prevailed, yet God gave hope. It seems a mystery, but creation knows it will be released from the bondage of death. It has to do with redemption brought through Jesus Christ. Creation was subjected to futility (death), not willingly but in hope (Rom. 8:19–20). Hope groans in our bodies (which are subject to sickness, injury, and death) for release—life beyond death. In Jesus Christ we are saved in this hope (the hope of resurrection) (Rom. 8:24).

We know much about deliverance from death because God revealed it to us through our resource, the Bible. When we read about Jesus Christ in the New Testament and the will of God, it all becomes clear.

Adam, however, knew one thing—that somehow or another, Abel was with God and he, Adam, and his wife, Eve, would be with Abel again. This understanding became incorporated into world religions practiced among the descendants of Adam. We see it, for example, in the pharaohs of Egypt with their great pyramids and the preparation they made by having items placed with loved ones in their burial for life in another world.

Just as Lamech in Genesis 4:16–24 knew the story of Cain five generations earlier, the descendants of Noah, in the earlier years of our planet, knew about Enoch, seven generations from Adam—Enoch who was and was not because God took him (Gen. 5:24 NIV): "Enoch walked with God; then he was no more because God took him away." One could say earth's early occupants knew of life after death because they intuited it. It may have been a bit hazy after a number of generations, but following Enoch it was common knowledge that there was life after death. Adam, a son of God who walked with God, knew about heaven, the nature of God, of His love and grace, and Adam understood somewhat of God's promise. (God communicated these things to Adam, "in the beginning" – read Isaiah 40:21 and Isaiah 48:16-17).

The Sorrow of Adam and Eve

Adam's gaze, as he moved his head circularly from the left to the right, took in the perspective of the leveled space, various trees for shade, some with fruit and neatly planted floral arrangements, with three attractive dwellings directly to his front. Eve, his beloved, stood in the doorway of the building to the right, her left hand braced against the door frame, staring. She looked faint, like she was going to fall, as she had numerous times before. Again she began to sob uncontrollably.

"Abel," she said. "Oh, my son Abel. I cannot believe you are gone. So this is death. It is cruel. A son is not supposed to die before his mother. Oh Lord God, it cannot be. Tell me it isn't so. Please let it be a lie. Abel, come home."

Adam joined her, his left arm around her. "Oh Abel," said Adam, "my son Abel. Would to God that it could have been me slain rather than you, righteous Abel, oh righteous Abel. I cannot believe it. Yet it is true."

He pulled Eve to him, and she wept on his right shoulder. This was something new. There had been no tears in the garden. When they left the garden, they had cried together for many days. Now they both wept uncontrollably.

They turned and joined hands, walking together to the east, as they had done time and time again. Wolf, Abel's dog, followed them, whimpering.

They were silent now. After some minutes, they approached a large, flat rock where they did their winnowing.

"Look," said Eve, "there is Abel's flock, standing silently before his altar. His twelve sheep have done this the last ten days since his disappearance. See how mysteriously they stand, as if in his honor. Surely Elohim directs their thoughts."

"And, there is Cain's altar just to the south," said Adam. "Perhaps Cain wanted Abel's place. Abel built his altar first. Didn't I instruct both of them to worship God, and didn't I tell them they needed to be clothed? I never thought worshipping Elohim would lead to murder."

Eve started to cry again. They turned to the east, looking into the valley and over to the adjacent mount.

"Oh, Cain, my son Cain," said Eve, "Why did you kill your brother? Did you not know that we love you? Elohim loves you. Why have you fled?"

"Did you notice," said Adam, "a stone missing from Cain's altar? Evette said Cain hit Abel in the head with it."

"Where is Abel's body?" cried Eve. She asked it over and over.

Adam patiently replied, "Evette said Cain hid it in the ground somewhere over the side of the mount—to the east. Now all three are gone—Abel dead, in the ground, Cain and Evette to the great river to the east," said Adam. "We will start again. But I fear Cain has started a new thing—hate and murder. We must do different. We must be for peace. We will have more children. And we will have a new beginning. We'll call this place Salem."

35

Suffering

Adam and Eve had two groupings of children. Adam and Eve lost their first children through no fault of their own. They lost not only Abel, but they lost Cain and a daughter as well. Cain moved off to a place called Nod, meaning the place of the vagabond or fugitive—a location east of Eden (Gen. 4:16). Cain took with him a daughter of Adam and Eve, for he knew his wife and she bore Enoch (Gen. 4:17). There Cain and his wife had children, grandchildren, and great-grandchildren. In fact, Cain built a city and named it after his firstborn, Enoch, meaning "well regulated" (Gen. 4:17). (It would be Cain's Eden, Utopia!)

The human race, resulting from the fall, would experience sorrow in childbirth (Gen. 3:16). God said to Eve, "I will greatly multiply your sorrow and your conception; in pain you shall bring forth children." In addition to pain in conception came the death of children and sorrow in the birthing process. Eve, I think, with perfect health didn't lose children in childbirth.

But as time went on, it would be a common experience to lose a child at birth, and sometimes a woman would die while giving birth. Rachel, the wife of Jacob, a grandson of Abraham, died while she was giving birth to a son, Benjamin (Gen. 35:16–20).

In addition, due to various diseases, many children would die at an early age. Humankind would undergo suffering, misery, and great distress. One example is in the life of Thomas Jefferson, the third president of the United States, and his wife Martha. At eighteen Martha married Bathurst Skelton. By nineteen she was widowed, and her son by Bathurst died before his fourth birthday. In ten years of marriage to Thomas, she birthed six children. A son and two daughters died as infants. Their fourth child died in her second year from whooping cough. Two daughters, Martha and Marie, lived. Mrs. Jefferson died from complications birthing her last daughter, Maria. Maria died before her father, President Jefferson.[86]

God, starting with Adam, has taught mankind the consequences of estrangement from Him. At the same time we learn that our loving God gives a future to people who place their trust in Him. For those who are reconciled to God, we are promised that He will wipe away every tear from our eyes. In our life with the Father through Jesus Christ in the celestial, "There will be no more death, nor sorrow, nor crying, nor will there be any more pain" (Rev. 21:4). Those things will all have passed away. We will return to a life without suffering, the kind Adam and Eve had known in the garden.

Adam, however, knew his disobedience had created an environment of suffering not only for his own family but for the millions upon millions who were to come. Not only was he laden with guilt over estrangement from God and his removal from Eden but also for his family malaise. Murder had come into the world. A child, grown, was intended to leave his or her home and be joined to a spouse, thus starting a new family (Gen. 2:21–25). Even so, there should always be a healthy connection to one's family of origin. Adam found himself not only estranged from God but also from a son and a daughter, Cain and Cain's wife. Adam's family life with his first family was tragic, worse than dysfunctional.

---

86 David L. Holmes, *The Faiths of the Founding Fathers*. (Oxford, NY: Oxford University Press, Inc., 2006,), 121–5.

Adam and Eve suffered spiritually and mentally. They also suffered physically. We don't know the extent of their physical suffering. For sure, Adam and Eve eventually died physically (Gen. 5:5). So it was in the beginning, and so it will be on planet earth until the Lord Jesus gives us a new world.

36

Spirituality

Adam and Eve personally knew God, had an empirical faith. They had talked with God and walked with Him in the garden. Transitioning from a relationship in which they knew God with their physical senses they now had to live by faith. Their family would have to live by faith and all people who descended from them. The new criterion God required is clearly enunciated in the New Testament Hebrews 11:6 (NIV): "And without faith it is impossible to please God, because anyone who comes to him must believe that He exists, and that he rewards those who earnestly seek Him."

Adam and Eve of course believed in God. They could not in good conscience fail to believe in Him because they knew for a fact from their existence and previous experience that God did exist. The action God took in clothing them with animal skins meant they were in a favorable relationship with Him and were recipients of His grace, in hope of redemption. Evidently they were diligently seeking Him, endeavoring to please Him, and doing His will because they taught their sons, Abel and Cain to make sacrifices to Him. In all this we see Adam and Eve met the specifications of Hebrews 11:6, and although it wasn't written until many years later, it was always the plan God had for men and women to please Him in Christ.

The history of mankind presenting sacrifices and offerings to God began with Abel and Cain (Gen. 4:4–5). This practice goes all the way back to the beginning. We may assume Adam and Eve did the same. We know for sure the first humans born on earth did so because our resource gives information about it. Cain and Abel are referenced specifically because of a conflict that arose in which Cain's offering was not accepted, an incident that led to the murder of his brother Abel.

It's possible the occasion was Cain's first attempt at such worship. Abel probably made many such offerings because in Hebrews 11:4 we read, "He was righteous, God testifying of his gifts." Note the word *gifts* is in the plural. Abel's offerings were regularly accepted. When Cain took the initiative, joining his brother in this faith venture, it did not go well for him. His undertaking was the first in world history of all that was to follow in the way of illegitimate religion, an imitation of the legitimate.

It's significant to observe that Cain and Abel were taught about God. It is the obligation of parents to have a home in which the Lord is honored and to teach their children about God. Cain and Abel worshipped the Lord that is the Son of God. Obviously the boys knew the promise of Genesis 3:15. They knew about the clothing of Adam and Eve. It's the reason later that we see both Cain and Abel presenting offerings to God. The truth of God, His existence, presence and providence, love, and grace and our need of His blessing is so overwhelmingly manifest that there is nowhere one can go on earth to escape this reality.

Today we do not offer sacrifices to God like that of Cain and Abel. Jesus made the one sacrifice for us (Christians) by which we are acceptable to God. "We have been sanctified through the offering of the body of Jesus once for all" (Heb. 10:10). The offering Abel made foreshadowed and prophetically pointed to the one made by Jesus, the sacrifice made on the cross that in effect takes away our sin and makes us right with God. Another reason we have an account of Cain and Abel's offering is because God wanted it on record that His intention was to save us

37

Blood

Adam taught Cain and Abel that God would provide a Seed, to destroy Satan and his work, meaning sin and death. The result for mankind would be paradise regained in an afterlife with God. Access would come through the promised person born out of a woman. God also taught Adam and Eve that they needed to be clothed. The clothes God gave them made of animal skins required the death of an animal. The death of an animal involved the shedding of blood. The message of our resource is the same throughout. We are made right with God through the shedding of blood.

Both the Law in the Old Testament and the New Testament teach purification by blood; "without the shedding of blood there is no forgiveness" (Heb. 9:22 NIV). Those who are right with God were chosen in Jesus "before the creation of the world" (Eph. 1:4 NIV). Reading on, it is confirmed "in Him [Jesus Christ] we have redemption through His blood, the forgiveness of sins, in accordance with the riches of God's grace" (Eph. 1:7 NIV).

The promise in Genesis 3:15 has to do with God's coming to us through the woman, Mary (Matt.1:18–23). Jesus, born of Mary, never sinned, lived a perfect life, and shed His blood outside Jerusalem on the cross of Calvary. It is through Him that we are saved.

Adam taught Cain and Abel to make a blood sacrifice through which they would declare their belief in the coming one. He would forgive sins through His blood. Cain did his own thing and made an offering of produce, which he gathered from his horticulture. Abel offered a lamb, a blood offering, declaring his faith in the person God determined to be our Savior. God was pleased with Abel's offering. Abel by faith looked to Christ Jesus.

"By faith Abel offered God a more excellent sacrifice than Cain, through which he obtained witness that he was righteous, God testifying of his gifts; and through it he being dead still speaks" (Heb. 11:4). First, Abel's offering was a sacrifice. Second, it was made by faith—that is, belief in the coming One he was taught about by Adam. Third, it was a more excellent sacrifice, a forerunner to all the others made by Noah, Abraham, those under the Law, and on the cross by Christ, all meaning we are made right with God through Jesus and Jesus alone (John 14:6). Fourth, Abel's sacrifice indicated he was righteous, also prefiguring the teaching of justification by faith as taught by the apostle Paul in the book of Romans. Fifth, Abel, though he is dead, through his offering still speaks. Hebrews 11:4 informs us Abel's offering has a message.

The proclamation, paramount in the theme of Hebrews, concerning the superiority of Christ, and the message of Romans concerning justification by faith is that one is forgiven of his or her sin through the blood of Jesus. That person is declared righteous with the righteousness of Christ as a free gift by God's grace through faith in Jesus Christ, the Son of God.

> But now the righteousness of God apart from the law is revealed, being witnessed by the law and the Prophets, even the righteousness of God, through faith in Jesus Christ, to all and on all who believe. For there is no difference; for all have sinned and fall short of the glory of God, being justified freely by His grace through the redemption that is in Christ Jesus, whom God set forth as a propitiation by His blood, through faith, to demonstrate

His righteousness, because in His forbearance God had passed over the sins that were previously committed, to demonstrate at the present time His righteousness, that He might be just and the justifier of the one who has faith in Jesus, (Rom. 3:21–26)

Cain did not give glory to God or recognize the Son of God. He did not offer what God required but offered what he, Cain, felt like offering. Cain was out of sync with the prophecy in Genesis 3:15, the teaching of his father, Adam, and the acceptable sacrifice of Abel. His action was inconsistent with all that is taught about the purpose of sacrifice in the rest of the Bible in all of these particulars, and he did not acknowledge the will of God.

The Scripture, our resource, teaches in Hebrews 12:23–24 that Abel made a blood sacrifice. But the blood Abel offered, while prophetically pointing to our need to be saved by blood, did not save or get people into fellowship with God. It is specifically the blood of Jesus that is the God-determined required blood sacrifice by which we are made right with God. Only the blood of the Son of God is an acceptable offering to take away sin. It is not only better than the blood Abel offered, the blood of an animal, which has no moral quality to it, but the blood of Jesus is also the exclusive means to salvation. Note, in the Son of God, Jesus, the Savior, the writer of Hebrews states,

> You have come to God, the judge of all men, to the spirits of righteous men made perfect, to Jesus the mediator of a new covenant, and to the sprinkled blood that speaks a better word than the blood of Abel. (Heb. 12:22–24 NIV)

38

Portent

The story of Adam and Eve their sons and immediate posterity present one unified picture as we trace the history of mankind in our resource and secular history through time to our present day. The center of everything is the promised Deliverer of Genesis 3:15. In the beginning God—Elohim, the Father, the Son, and the Holy Spirit—created the heavens and the earth (Gen. 1:1). The Lord God, *Yahwah* Elohim, the Son of God, who was later born as a human, Jesus, is first specifically referenced in Genesis 2:5.

"*Ya*" O and "*huwa*" he, "O He," the "He" of Genesis 3:15 who spoke to Satan in Genesis 3:15 is the He who would come of a woman and bruise Satan's head. Yahweh, according to one viewpoint, was originally a finite causative verb from the Northwest Semitic root hwy "to be, to come into being," so that this divine name means "he causes to be, or exists" (i.e., "he creates").[87]

That is how He is presented by the apostle John in John 1:1–3.

> In the beginning was the Word, and the Word was with God, and the Word was God. He was in the beginning with God. All things were made through Him, and without Him nothing was made that was made.

---

87   Merrill F. Unger, *Unger's Bible Dictionary.* (Chicago: Moody Press, 1970), 1177.

The apostle Paul presents Jesus in the same way. He writes,

> For by Him all things were created that are in heaven and
> that are on earth, visible and invisible, whether thrones
> or dominions or principalities or powers. All things were
> created through Him and for Him. And He is before all
> things, and in Him all things consist. (Col. 1:16–18)

Cain and Abel made offerings to Yahweh. Cain's worship was rejected. Abel's worship was accepted. Henceforth all mankind on planet earth would be divided into two groups—those for the Creator, the Son of God, the Lord Jesus, and those against the Creator, the Son of God, the Lord Jesus. It should not surprise us that some argue against a creation and oppose the Lord God of Adam and Eve.

The struggle between these two groups will go on until the Son of God comes through the heavens, returning to planet earth in a time of judgment. We see it in Psalm 1, approximately in the middle of the Scripture, presented as the way of the righteous as over and against the way of the ungodly.

At the death of Jesus, the Savior, Yahweh, in the flesh, we recognize the same division. Jesus died upon a cross outside Jerusalem at a place called Golgotha—that is to say the place of the Skull. "Two robbers were crucified with Him, one on the right and one on his left" (Matt. 27:38 NIV). Both robbers heaped insults on Jesus, calling Him names, as did the crowd beneath the cross (Matt. 27:44 NIV). The apostle John reminds us that Jesus was in the center of the robbers (John 19:18). At one point, as those crucified suffered, one of the robbers had a change of heart and rebuked the other for his harsh words against Jesus. He said,

> Do you not even fear God, seeing you are under the same
> condemnation? And we indeed justly, for we receive the
> due reward of our deeds; but this Man has done noth-
> ing wrong. Then he said to Jesus, "Lord," remember me

when You come into Your kingdom. And Jesus said to him, Assuredly, I say to you today you will be with Me in Paradise. (Luke 23:40–43)

The other robber did not repent. It was the story of Cain and Abel all over again. The person who by faith called on Jesus for mercy ended up with Him in Paradise, God's Eden at that time. The man who did not recognize the Lord God did not end up in Paradise. This picture is so important that the Spirit of God, in Isaiah 53, guiding the prophet Isaiah as he prophesied about the death of Jesus on the cross six hundred years before it happened, specified Jesus would be numbered with transgressors (Isa. 53:12)—that is, Jesus would be crucified among criminals. The significance of this historical event is it follows through with the portent of Abel and Cain illustrating until the Second Coming of Jesus mankind will be divided into those for the Lord and those against the Lord.

39

Cain

Cain, the firstborn of Adam, has the historic distinction of being the first human born on planet earth. Adam was the first created, but Cain the first born. Spiros Zodhiates, ThD, writes, "It is possible that Cain and Abel were twins, because the text does not repeat the statement that Eve conceived."[88] (See Gen. 4:1–2.)

It's sensible to believe that Cain and Abel, as all siblings, experienced competition. It is highly probable that Abel pleased Adam and Eve with his attitude and behavior while Cain often did not. The apostle John, sometimes called the apostle of love in the New Testament, wrote, "This is the message you heard from the beginning: We should love one another" (1 John 3:11 NIV). He wrote about the love he was taught by Jesus from the beginning of their relationship. Jesus teaches us to love one another. Such, of course, was taught by Adam to his sons. God, who Adam knew well, is love (1 John 4:16). John contrasts an admonition to love with those who do not love by making a reference to Cain. John wrote,

> We should love one another, not as Cain who was of
> the wicked one and murdered his brother. And why did

---

88 Spiros Zodhiates, complier and editor, *Hebrew Greek Key Study Bible*, (Iowa Falls, IA: World Bible Publisher, 1988), 6.

he murder him? Because his works were evil and his brother's righteous. (1 John 3:11–12)

The apostle John tells us Abel was righteous, which means he did what God wanted him to do. He also tells us that Cain was of the wicked one, which is to say his attitude and behavior were fueled by thoughts he received from Satan. In context John tells us Abel was a person characterized by love. Cain was the opposite, meaning he was indifferent to God. Cain's spirit would indicate he was also indifferent to his parents, Adam and Eve. Appreciation for God and respect for authority go together.

John also informs us that Cain killed his brother Abel because Cain's works were evil and Abel's works were righteous. We are definitely taught those doing evil hate those doing righteousness. Some people are despised because their activity is good. Those who do not do good hate those who do. That's why all who try to live godly lives will suffer persecution (2 Tim. 3:12).

John was contrasting Cain and Abel to teach about love and hate. Going on from verses 11 and 12, John wrote,

> Do not marvel, my brethren, if the world hates you. We know that we have passed from death to life, because we love the brethren. He who does not love the brethren is a murderer, and you know that no murderer has eternal life abiding in him. (1 John 3:13–15)

Someone has said that hate is not the opposite of love. Indifference is the opposite of love. Cain was cold toward God, and we can suppose he was the same toward his parents. Cain's anger at the favor shown Abel had turned to hatred, eating away at his soul until God's acceptance of Abel's offering and rejection of his offering eventuated into physical violence against Abel, which resulted in Abel's termination.

Favor, by the way, is a natural response to someone truly loving and respecting others. Sin lies at the door of one full of jealousy, perverseness, insincerity, greed, and maliciousness. Such was the way of Cain. Jude, one of the brothers of Jesus (Mark 6:3), instructed about those who serve Satan in opposition to God. "Woe to them!" he wrote, "They have taken the way of Cain" (Jude 11 NIV). Cain's way is just that—it's Cain's way and not God's way. The writer of Proverbs wrote, "A man who isolates himself seeks his own desire; he rages against all wise judgment" (Prov. 18:1). Cain's way is the beginning of vagabonds who isolate themselves from others because they want to do their own thing.

Cain's way determined the direction humans on planet earth would live. There were those who would seek peace and serve God, the true God, the Creator, in the best way they knew how. Others mobilized, forcibly confiscating land, women, horses, and the possessions of meek or weaker people. Such would make up stories or myths to justify their licentious worship. They would fashion gods in their image and use them to enslave others, building kingdoms for their god, Satan. Cain's punishment for fratricide was a defiled land that would no longer yield its strength (Gen. 4:9–12) (hence his need to invent gods that would bring fertility to the land). Cain was to be a fugitive (live in disgrace from others) and a vagabond (not really be part of what God was going to do with planet earth). Cain's response to God was, "My punishment is more than I can bear!" (Gen. 4:13 NIV). Cain did not repent, change his mind about his actions, or have any remorse.

Cain accepted his status. He didn't ask for mercy (forgiveness for what he had done) or for grace (undeserved favor) (Gen. 4:14). He said, "It will happen that anyone who finds me will kill me" (Gen. 4:14). In other words, in the future, sons of Adam will look for me to avenge Abel. So be it. Cain's statement meant, "Let others from Adam come against me. There will be combat." The idea was, "Whoever comes after me will get what Abel got."

The Lord answered Cain, "If anyone kills Cain, he will suffer vengeance seven times over" (Gen. 4:15 NIV). Why did the Lord not send someone out to kill Cain? Because the Lord did not want mankind involved in war in which people, created beings, were killing other people made in the image of God.

"The Lord put a mark on Cain so that no one who found him would kill him" (Gen. 4:15 NIV). I'm claiming Jeremiah 33:3 (NIV) to understand the mystery of the mark: "Call to me and I will answer you and tell you great and unsearchable things you do not know." It may be the mark of Cain was not a physical mark on his body. Cain had the stigma of being identified as a murderer. Is there anything worse than being known as a murderer? Being a murderer is a mark of shame.

Yet Cain and his posterity could get away with murder and live acceptable among humankind.

The City of Man, Cain's city, Enoch (Gen. 4:17), as opposed to the City of God, the coming Zion (Heb. 11:8–10), would sanction murder, the killing of others, through war as a natural process for empire building. Today we believe there is a just war. But war too often has been glorified, and Cain's way, fratricide, in history through great empires and military conquerors has been lauded.

40

Abel

Abel (breath, like the Spirit of God), diametrically different than Cain, was the second son of Adam and Eve, the second man born on planet earth. It would have been interesting if Cain and Abel had been identical twins. The contrast between the two clearly illustrates moral distinction in character.

When Samuel, a prophet (man of God), was sent to anoint a king, someone from the house of Jesse, he was impressed with Eliab, the firstborn son. He thought, surely the Lord's anointed, the one to be king, is before me. But God said not to look at his appearance, or at his physical stature. "The Lord does not look at the things man looks at. Man looks at the outward appearance, but the Lord looks at the heart." (I Sam. 16:7 NIV) David, from whom Jesus Christ descended, was anointed king. He was a man after God's own heart.

Abel, who had a heart for God, heads the list of God's faith heroes in Hebrews 11. Men and women referenced there are honored as people who pleased God. They are in God's Hall of Fame. They are excellent examples of what it means to live by faith—trust in the Son of God. It is written,

> It was by faith that Abel brought a more acceptable offer-
> ing to God than Cain did. Abel's offering gave evidence

that he was a righteous man, and God showed his approval of his gifts. Although Abel is long dead, he still speaks to us by his example of faith. (Heb. 11:4 NLT)

It is clear God's faith history does not begin with Abraham, Moses, and the Law or in the New Testament but with righteous Abel. The beginning is in the beginning.

Abel recognized God, worshipped Him, and presented an offering to Him. Abel's offering or sacrifice was declared by God to be excellent. It was excellent because by faith he acknowledged in his offering that he could only be justified—pronounced not guilty of his sin—through the person of the Son of God, Jesus Christ. It is only through the blood of Jesus that we are forgiven of our sin. This teaching constitutes the teaching of the Bible from the beginning to the end. Abel, and other early men, far superior to us in intelligence, grasped clearly that they were dependent upon God for everything.

All who are justified, beginning with Abel, from every dispensation are justified through the Son of God, who we know as Jesus Christ. Naturally, Abel didn't have as much detail as we have about Jesus. He did not know Lord God, the Son of God, as the human Jesus. But he did know his redemption would come through a man born of woman and that he needed to be clothed with the goodness of God to cover his nakedness. The human Jesus, as the Son of God, knew Abel from the very beginning. When the offering of Abel was accepted, it meant Abel's faith was accepted.

Abel's sacrifice gave witness that he was righteous. Abel was righteous because by trusting in the Son of God, Abel received the merit of Jesus Christ, the righteousness of Jesus, as a free gift. The apostle Paul taught righteousness comes to those who believe in Jesus, the Son of God, for salvation. In Romans 4:3 Paul used a believer like Abel to demonstrate how we get righteous. "For what does the Scripture say? Abraham believed God and it was credited to him as righteousness." (NIV)

God testifies to us about the acceptability of Abel's "gifts." Yes, Abel offered more sacrifices than one. His sacrifices or gifts were later required by the Law. The Law is our tutor, instruction, to bring us to Christ, "that we might be justified by faith" (Gal. 3:24).

It's been six thousand years since Abel, but the sacrifice of Abel still speaks. Abel's witness, through his sacrifice, demonstrates the sufficiency of Jesus Christ as our Savior. That's what the book of Hebrews is all about.

> God who at various times and in various ways spoke in times past to the fathers by the prophets, has in these last days spoken to us by His Son, whom He has appointed heir of all things, through whom also He made the worlds, who being the brightness of His glory, and the express image of His person, and upholding all things by the word of His power, When he had by Himself purged our sins, sat down at the right hand of the Majesty on high. (Heb. 1:1–3)

The faith of Abel at the dawn of history, called to our attention in Hebrews 11:4, enlightens us about the singular purpose of God in Jesus Christ. Early believers did understand the basics about how to trust in their Creator, the Lord God, to please Him and to gain access to Him. Abel and those of kindred belief sought to know about God and the things of God. Jude notes of Enoch, the seventh generation from Adam, that Enoch prophesied about the second coming of Jesus Christ. Such is astounding, a phenomenal perception at such an early date. Jude wrote, "Enoch, the seventh from Adam, prophesied about these men: See, the Lord is coming with thousands upon thousands of his holy ones to judge everyone" (Jude 14–15 NIV).

Not only was Abel the first human born on planet earth to get back into a right relationship with God, but he was also the first martyr. The apostle John taught that the unrighteous hate the righteous. What was true of Cain has been true of those of his persuasion through all time.

Jesus spoke about His Father having a vineyard that He lent out to vinedressers. The vinedressers did not recognize the owner or pay Him what they owed. The vineyard owner would send servants to collect.

> The vinedressers took his servants, beat one, killed one, and stoned another. Again he sent other servants, more than the first, and they did likewise to them. Then last of all he sent his son to them, saying, "they will respect my son." But when the vinedressers saw the son, they said, among themselves, "This is the heir. Come, let kill him and seize his inheritance." So they took him and cast him out of the vineyard and killed him. (Matt. 21:35–39)

Jesus, the Son of God, "was in the world, and though the world was made through Him, the world did not recognize Him" (John 1:10 NIV). "He came to His own, and His own did not receive Him" (John 1:11). The world did not accept Jesus because He was righteous. Like Cain, the people of the world, Jew and Gentile, murdered Jesus, the Son of God.

So Jesus said to those of Cain's stripe, the religious leaders of Jerusalem,

> I send you prophets, wise men, and scribes; some of them you will kill and crucify, and some of them you will scourge in your synagogues and persecute from city to city, that on you may come all the righteous blood shed on the earth from the blood of righteous Abel to the blood of Zechariah, son of Berechiah, whom you murdered between the temple and altar. (Matt. 23:34–35)

Cain is marked as the first murderer in human history, a stubborn, unrepentant vagabond, the prototype of all who insist the universe is all there is. Abel is recorded by that which is called in Daniel 10:21 the Book of Truth (NIV), our resource, the Scripture, as a person of faith, accepted of God, the first human born on earth among those known as the people of God. His gifts give testimony to the truth that he pleased God. Jesus mentioned Abel as a real person in history who was a martyr, a man to whom was imputed righteousness.

Matthew, an apostle of Jesus, records the remark by Jesus about Abel, listing him essentially as the first prophet, along with all the others, the martyrs, up to Zechariah, the prophet. Good things are recorded concerning Abel, the son of Adam and Eve. The writer of the book of Hebrews, who heralds Abel in God's hall of famous believers, teaches us Abel "by faith . . . still speaks, even though he is dead" (Heb. 11:4 NIV).[89] Hurrah for Abel!

---

89 Augustine taught that Abel prefigured that society of men who say, "But I am like a green olive tree in the house of God: I have trusted in the mercy of God." In other words, Abel speaks for the City of God and is the first, born of man, who was a vessel of honor, placing his hope in God. Ibid., 302.

41

Faith

Adam and Eve were made right with God by the Son of God through faith. When the Lord God made tunics of skins for Adam and Eve and clothed them (Gen. 3:21), He indicated they were imputed righteousness through faith.[90]

God's method of receiving people through the Son of God *by faith* began with Adam. Hence Adam's son Abel came to God through the testimony of his parents, Adam and Eve. Abel then is listed as the first among those who followed the faith method to get righteousness (Heb. 11:4). It is clearly taught that without faith it is impossible to please God. "He who comes to God must believe that He is" (Heb. 11:6).

Adam's and Eve's faith was empirical. Adam knew God personally as his Creator. Adam and Eve heard God's voice audibly, and they visibly saw His aura. They walked with God in the garden in the cool of the evening, communicating with Him. Their knowledge was not philosophical. They didn't have to reason to prove their own being (I think therefore I am). They received specific verbal instruction from God, distinct revelation.

---

90 The subject of Adam and Eve being clothed is explained in chapter 23, "Clothing."

For us to understand God, we must study the content revealed about Him in His resource, the Bible, from the beginning to the very end, from Genesis to Revelation. True, we don't experience God the way Adam knew Him, but here in the beginning, with Abel and Cain and their parents, we get a clear understanding about what the Bible means by faith.

Cain and Abel worshipped God through testimony given to them about God. Because of Adam's sin, the relationship between mankind and God had been ruptured. God did not speak to Cain and Abel or manifest Himself to them prior to Abel's sacrifices.

Cain and Abel both believed in the existence of God. They had no reason to doubt their parents. Abel had a faith that connected him with God. Cain did not please God. In other words, Cain did not have faith. Cain's lack of faith was not based on a belief that God did not exist. David Platt in his excellent book, *Radical* in chapter 7, "There is No B Plan," writes:

1. All People Have Knowledge of God
2. All People Reject God.[91]

(Platt then goes on with five additional points to teach that salvation is by faith through Jesus Christ.)

There was in Abel sin, a rejection of God, the idea to do his own thing, but he made a decision to act on the knowledge given to him by Adam about God, to recognize the Son of God in blood sacrifice, and to seek forgiveness for his sin. It was counted to him for righteousness or saving faith. Cain, on the other hand, did not have faith because he rejected the will of God.

Having biblical faith involves a moral response to one's knowledge of God and God's will for one's life. It has to do with a choice to do God's

---

91 David Platt, *Radical*. (Colorado Springs, CO: Multnomah Books, 2010), 141–60.

will—obedience. Rejecting God and His will keeps one in a state of nonbelief.

Lee Strobel in his incredibly good book *The Case for Faith* recollects a high school biology class in which Charles Darwin's theory removed for him intellectually the last remnants he had of faith in God.[92] Further in his book he writes, truthfully,

> I was ... happy to latch onto Darwinism as an excuse to jettison the idea of God so I could unabashedly pursue my own agenda in life without moral constraints.[93]

The Lord Jesus, God, who requires faith as the proper response to His death on the cross, taught, "For God so loved the world He gave His only begotten Son, that whoever believes in Him should not perish but have everlasting life" (John 3:16). Jesus then went on to give us a psychology of faith.

> For God did not send His Son into the world to condemn the world, but that the world through Him might be saved. He who believes in Him is not condemned; but he who does not believe is condemned already because he has not believed in the name of the only begotten Son of God. And this is the condemnation that light has come into the world, and men loved darkness rather than light, because their deeds were evil. For everyone practicing evil hates the light and does not come to the light, lest his deeds be exposed. But he who does the truth comes to the light, that his deeds may be clearly seen, that they have been done in God. (John 3:17–21)

The Holy Spirit, through the writing of the apostle Paul, teaches in Romans 10:17, "Faith comes by hearing and hearing by the word of

---

92 Lee Strobel, *The Case For Faith*. (Grand Rapids, MI: Zondervan, 2000), 89.

93 Ibid., 91.

God." Cain and Abel heard the same message from Adam and Eve. Cain rejected it, and Abel accepted it. That is, Cain rejected God, the Son of God; and Abel obeyed God, the Son of God.

David Platt teaches, "All People Have Knowledge of God." I concur. Jesus is the Light of men (John 1:4), the Light that shines in the darkness (John 1:5), the true Light that "gives light to every man [human being] coming into the world" (John 1:9). As already noted, a human being is a spirit living in a body. Every human born on earth has innate light, through Jesus, the Spirit of God, who intuits to his or her spirit an awareness of God. Coming to God through Jesus by faith is not an intellectual process. It's a spiritual one. Abel was spiritually open to the leading of God's Holy Spirit to become a believer. Cain, following the Devil in darkness, became a murderer and then a liar.

According to the apostle Paul, God's existence is clearly perceived through the glory of His creation. The truth of His righteousness, moral rectitude, has been corrupted by those who live in unbelief.

> What may be known of God is manifest in them, for God has shown it to them. For since the creation of the world His invisible attributes are clearly seen, being understood by the things that are made, even His eternal power and Godhead, so that they [who chose not to believe] are without excuse. (Rom. 1:19–20)

While everyone knows there is a God, that knowledge in and of itself is not enough to bring a person into a saving relationship with God through His Son, Jesus. If one is to truly believe, the same God who gives innate knowledge about Himself and an appreciation for His creation must illuminate that person's spirit about Himself and His will through His Spirit by special revelation, the Word. Abel, demonstrated true belief by acting on the revelation he received through his parents, the Word, and was declared by God not guilty of his sin and right with God. Faith does not come from an intellectual community. Faith comes through the

Spirit of God. Saving faith is evidenced by our compliance with God's will, obedience as revealed in His Word.

Hebrews 11:6 informs us that faith has to do with believing God is and that He rewards those who diligently seek Him. God, who rejected Cain's offering, in so doing indicated Cain was not seeking Him. Cain's disbelief, like all disbelief, was a matter of choice. The Scripture clearly teaches that failure to believe is an unacceptable moral choice. People in ignorance about God need to be taught. Many do not make an Abel-type decision because of misunderstanding. Such is particularly true due to the teaching of a false religion or various anti-God philosophies. But emphatically, all people originally know there is a God. Understand, then, that unbelief in a person is rebellion against God, wherein a man or woman is not doing what God wants to be done. Also understand that *not believing in God*, whether in atheism, agnosticism, or skepticism, is a taught immoral animosity against God.

Lee Strobel, who had been an atheist because of Darwin's teaching on evolution, notes in *The Case for Faith* that he became a seeker of the truth. He wrote, "My training in journalism and law compels me to dig beneath opinion, speculation, and theories, all the way down until I hit the bedrock of solid facts."[94] It was Strobel's search for truth that led him to faith in Christ Jesus. Thus he gives us marvelous testimony to the Son of God by writing excellent books on the case for Christ, Jesus, creation, faith, Easter, and the resurrection. I highly recommend all his books.

There are many like Lee Strobel (C. S. Lewis comes to mind) who are nonbelievers who have come to faith in Christ Jesus. Their sojourn, as well as the confusion many have as a result at being misled or never having been taught from the Scripture about our Creator, enlightens us that it imperative for Christians to do the best they can to get the truth out about the reality of God, Jesus Christ, and His will for our lives.

---

94   Ibid.

Some thoughts on this subject are in order. The idea that the existence of God must be scientifically proven is totally invalid. God is outside the realm of such inquiry. Statements like, "God cannot be proved but neither can He be disproved" are misleading. Such thinking is erroneous. This kind of conceptualism is imposed on believers by Darwinism. It presupposes materialism (i.e., all reality is physical). It is, of course, a false philosophy.

A person has a physical brain, but the thought processes of that brain are mental. We are more than physical beings composed of so many elements. We are spirits in bodies. The thing we call science has to do with studying the creation and how it works. God is outside the creation. Christian belief is that God made the creation. The position that God is above and beyond creation is a quintessential tenant of theistic belief others must concede if they want intelligent dialogue on belief. God Himself is not subject to scientific analysis. It's for that reason that God's existence is not subject to scientific study.

For the Christian, however, to enter discourse with an atheist within a mental framework of materialism, speaking about not being able to prove or disprove God is not only inaccurate but is to compromise with a presupposition that is at variance with God and the truth of His being. God is not measurable and neither can He be seen through a microscope or telescope. We don't prove or disprove God; He is. (Read Gen. 1:1).

The Christian does not need to present arguments for the existence of God to legitimize his or her belief. To do so is analogous to proving the existence of the sun to someone who wants to argue about it. I know the sun exists because I have personally seen it for thousands of days. A blind person who has been told the sun does exist by one person and that it does not exist by another might ask for testimony about it. Even though a blind person cannot see it, the sun's reality can be felt on a warm day. A Christian should not feel compelled to prove God's existence to anyone.

Nevertheless, we can share with another having a problem in this area that we personally know God exists. I have experienced the presence of Jesus Christ in my life, which means I know God empirically. He has given me love, joy, peace, longsuffering, kindness, goodness, faithfulness, gentleness, and self-control, fruit of the Holy Spirit (Gal. 5:22–23). When I became a Christian, I received new life. I changed. Others noticed the change, and some became Christians. I have seen how Christ changes people's lives and how He makes people better. This reality cuts through all philosophies of unbelief, no matter what they may be.

God has confirmed to me over and over multiple times, objectively, His presence and power through prayer. One example is what I saw Him do for an air force officer to whom I was ministering at an AFB in Mississippi. This man was in a situation where he needed to talk with his father. His predicament was impossible. He was not a Christian but was examining faith. I prayed with him that God would enable him to speak with his dad.

Following the prayer, the officer was assigned temporary duty in Kansas City. One evening while he was walking through his hotel lobby he met his dad, who was there on a business assignment. His dad lived in another state hundreds of miles away. By talking with his father, he was able to resolve a difficult situation.

When the officer returned to our base, he excitedly told me his story. He said, "God answered our prayer. That my father would be in the same state as me, staying in the same city, in the same hotel, on the same day, and that he would walk through the same lobby through which I was walking at the very same minute, is too much of a coincidence to think it was a random happening." This man was a scientific thinker who mentally studied the mathematical probability of whatever was being claimed. His experience with our specific prayer confirmed to him God's existence.

The Christian and nonbeliever are not on the same level playing field. The Christian says God exists. The atheist says God does not exist.

The Christian knows. The non-Christian will not acknowledge it. The Christian says he or she has experienced God. The non-Christian says he or she has not experienced God. The non-Christian attacks the concept of faith, saying the Christian is not scientific and does not act reasonably. But the non-Christian cannot disprove the Christian's claim. The best the non-Christian can say is, "I have not experienced God." It's all philosophical with the nonbeliever. The non-Christian has not disproved anything and does not know. The Christian knows. The Christian accepts the non-Christian's testimony of nothingness. The non-Christian cannot legitimately refute the Christian's testimony, for he or she in fact does not know what the Christian has experienced.

Faith is not a response to a religion. Religion is man's attempt to reach God through human effort. Cain tried that, but it was unacceptable. Faith has to do with God's love, mercy, and grace extended through the Son of God, Jesus Christ. Faith is relational. Faith for the believer begins, continues, and is ever with God the Father through Jesus the Son in the Holy Spirit.

Even though faith is essential to get connected with God, it is not our activity that gets us right with God. God gives the believer a new birth (John 3:3). The greatest miracle was not when God created the universe. The greatest miracle is when God takes a sinner and makes him or her into a saint.[95] Man cannot produce a spiritual birth. Spiritual newness in a person's life, a new heart, comes only from Christ in the Spirit through the power of our heavenly Father. Faith works for a person not because that person is good but because Jesus is good. We are made right with God, through the person of Jesus Christ, His perfect life, His death on the cross, and His resurrection from the dead.

---

95   This statement was made in a Hebrew class by Dr. Toyozo W. Nakarai.

42

Seth

Adam and Eve had a third son, Seth, which means "put" or "appointed." Knowledge of his birth and naming was furnished by Adam and Eve to Seth, passed along to his descendants and ultimately recorded as Genesis 4:25–26.

Eve, who named Seth, said, "For God has appointed another seed for me instead of Abel whom Cain killed" (Gen. 4:25). Cain could have been the seed of which Eve spoke, but Cain was not a man of faith. Adam and Eve were aware of his spirit and knew before he killed his brother Abel that he did not please God. A psychologist working out of a victim mentality might blame Cain's anger on bad interaction from over-demanding parents, but Cain was responsible for his attitude and his behavior. It was Abel who should have produced the Seed for whom Eve looked.

The point is that Eve was looking. She knew with Abel's death he was not the promised Seed, the one for whom she looked. The Seed for whom Eve was looking was the "He" God spoke about in Genesis 3:15. He was the Seed to be born of a woman. This was the Seed who would bruise the head of Satan and destroy his work, Satan's work being death and separation from God. The Seed for whom Eve looked was the promised Seed—the Savior of the world, Jesus Christ.

That Eve took Genesis 3:15 seriously and that she was seeking to do God's will by birthing the Seed or providing a righteous line from which the Seed could be born proves Eve was living by faith. Adam who knew Eve (sexually) (Gen. 4:25), like Abraham later in knowing Sarah, was working with her to produce the promised Seed. He too was living by faith.

Seth's seed, descendants, would now be the righteous line leading from Adam and Eve to the Seed who would save the world. See the genealogy of Jesus (Luke 3:23–38) from Mary back to Adam. Tracing Adam's descendants from Eve through the genealogies given in the Bible, we have the names of the people from whom the Christ is descended beginning with Abraham to Joseph, Mary's husband (Matt. 1:1–16).

Seth lived 105 years and begot a son named Enosh (Gen. 5:6). Enosh means "a man." By the time of Enosh, Adam and Eve probably concluded the promised Seed was not going to come immediately.

Whether Seth realized he was not the promised Seed or was impressed with his responsibility as a father, he and his family began to emphasize salvation: "Men began to call on the name of the Lord" (Gen. 4:26) (see Rom. 10:13).

"Men calling upon the Lord" refers to people worshipping the true and living God. Calling upon the name of the Lord, more specifically, is asking God for salvation (Acts 2:21). People calling upon God included Adam and Eve and some of their sons and daughters. Seth and Enosh calling upon the Lord is a precursor to Enoch (Gen. 5:24), Noah (Gen. 6:8–9, 7:1), and Abraham (Gen. 12:1–8) doing the same. Those, and others of faith, were people who worshipped the true and living God.

Adam lived during most of the lifetime of his son, Seth, and Enosh, his grandson. Adam lived 930 years (Gen. 5:3–5). Seth had sons and daughters (Gen. 5:7). Seth lived 912 years, and he died (Gen. 5:8). Enosh had sons and daughters (Gen. 5:10). Enosh lived 905 years, and he died (Gen. 5:11).

43

Genealogy

Adam has a genealogy of encompassment. It begins with Adam and his creation and extends to the life of Jesus Christ in the first century, including Christ's death, burial, and resurrection. Think about it—such documentation is phenomenal. The genealogy, written over a period of eighteen hundred years by various biblical writers, was completed almost two thousand years ago, a recent date compared to those who tell us the earth is over 4 billion years old. It begins with Adam (Gen. 5:1). It continues on with:

Seth (Gen. 5:3)
Enosh (Gen. 5:6)
Cainan (Gen. 5:9)
Mahalalel (Gen. 5:12)
Jared (Gen. 5:15)
Enoch (Gen. 5:18)
Methuselah (Gen. 5:21)
Lamech (Gen. 5:25)
Noah (Gen. 5:28–29)
Shem (Gen. 5:32)
Arphaxad (Gen. 11:10)
Salah (Gen. 11:12)
Eber (Gen. 11:14)

Peleg (Gen. 11:16)
Reu (Gen. 11:18)
Serug (Gen. 11:20)
Nahor (Gen. 11:22)
Terah (Gen. 11:24)

In Matthew 1:1, it continues with Abram (Gen. 11:26) and follows with:

Isaac (Gen. 21:3)
Jacob (Gen. 25:19–26)
Judah (Gen. 29:30–35)
Perez (Gen. 38:1–29)
Hezron (Gen. 46:12)
Ram (Ruth 4:19)
Amminadab (Ruth 4:19)
Nahson (Ruth 4:20)
Salmon (Ruth 4:20)
Boaz (Ruth 4:21)
Obed (Ruth 4:21)
Jesse (Ruth 4:22)
David, the king (Ruth 4:22)
Solomon (2 Sam. 12:24)
Rehoboam (1 Kings 11:43)
Abijah (1 Kings 14:31)
Asa (1 Kings 15:8)
Jehoshaphat (1 Kings 15:24)
Jehoram (1 Kings 22:50)
Uzziah (Matt. 1:9)
Jotham (Matt. 1:9)
Ahaz (2 Kings 16:2)
Hezekiah (2 Kings 16:20)
Manasseh (2 Kings 20:21)
Amon (2 Kings 21:18)
Josiah (2 Kings 21:23–26)

Jeconiah (2 Kings 23:34)

Jeconiah (2 Kings 24:6)

Shealtiel (Matt. 1:12)

Zerrubbabel (Ezra 3:2)

Abiud (Matt. 1:13)

Eliakim (Matt. 1:13)

Azor (Matt. 1:13)

Zadok (Matt. 1:14)

Akim (Matt. 1:14)

Eliud (Matt. 1:14)

Eleasar (Matt. 1:15)

Matthan (Matt. 1:15)

Jacob (Matt. 1:15)

Joseph (Matt. 1:16)

Jesus, the Christ, Anointed One (Matt. 1:16)

There are sixty-three generations from Adam through Jesus Christ.[96] If you count the believer who becomes a son of God or a daughter of God by adoption into the family of God through Jesus Christ, there are sixty-four generations from Adam to the person who inherits the promises of God as a joint-heir with Jesus Christ (Rom. 8:16–17).

Some folks who read the Bible skip the genealogies, muttering something about "boring." Every person, however, who is listed in a genealogy can

---

96   The genealogy of Jesus, which includes sixty-three generations, is that of His father Joseph in Matthew 1:1–16. Joseph was not the biological father of Jesus, Jesus being born of the virgin Mary (Matt. 1:18–25, Luke 1:26–35). Jesus was born of the Holy Spirit and is the Son of God (Luke 1:31–35). Joseph, however, graciously adopted Jesus as his own son (Matt. 1:18–25). I have used the genealogy of Jesus up to Joseph because the same way Joseph adopted Jesus as his son, thus receiving God as a human being, Jesus being born of Mary, God receives mankind through Jesus into His family as children of God (1 John 3:1–3), sons and daughters of God (2 Cor. 6:18). Every person born again through Jesus Christ has as his or her genealogy that given in the Bible from Adam to Abraham and from Abraham, recorded in Matthew, through Joseph to Jesus Christ. Jesus Christ begat us through the Holy Spirit to eternal life.

count it glory to be an ancestor of Christ Jesus. In addition, I like to think each person listed in Christ's genealogy is in a heavenly realm, still alive. The believer in Christ will one day meet each person, one by one, engaging in wondrous discussions about the details of life on earth and the privilege of a faith walk with the Lord.

Furthermore the genealogies impress us with the credibility of our resource, the Bible. God knew before He made our world what was going to happen (Eph. 1:3–14). From the very beginning, the Spirit guided His prophets to convey His message by word of mouth and through the written word in His predetermined plan for His only begotten Son to be born on planet earth and accomplish the purpose of redemption (2 Peter 1:16–21). We see this with Eve in Genesis 4:25 as she looks for the appointed seed—the "promised Seed" of Genesis 3:15.

What's the genealogy of Adam all about? The gospel writer Luke, guided by the Holy Spirit, traced the genealogy of Jesus Christ in Luke 3:23–38 back to Adam.[97] Luke in so doing is calling our attention to the promise God made to Adam and Eve, and to us, that one would be sent to destroy the work of Satan and to bring us back to paradise. The writer of Hebrews informs us about Jesus.

> Inasmuch, then as the children have partaken of flesh
> and blood, He Himself likewise shared in the same that
> though death He might destroy him who had the power
> of death, that is, the devil. (Heb. 2:14)

The genealogy in Luke 3 is that of Mary, mother of Jesus. Mary's genealogy is traced, as noted, back to Adam and thus Genesis 3:15 and

---

97 There are two genealogies of Jesus in the New Testament. The one in Matthew 1:1–16 is that of Joseph, the earthly father of Jesus, running prophetically from Abraham through King David to Joseph. The one in Luke 3:13–38 runs prophetically in the opposite direction from Mary back through David, and Abraham to Adam, demonstrating the fulfillment of Genesis 3:15, the promised one being born through the woman Mary.

the promise to bring a Savior through a woman, illustrating the perfect unity of God's plan as we follow it through the history of the Bible. From Adam to Mary, God worked His predetermined plan to bring redemption in Jesus. The Luke 3 genealogy runs through King David. Mary was a physical descendant of King David. This means that Jesus, as a son of Mary, is qualified to be the king of the Jews. Jesus is the Anointed One, Christ (King), and the Messiah (King) of Israel.[98]

---

98 Jesus, meaning "Savior," was the name of the Lord. Christ, meaning "King," is a transliteration of the Greek word for king. Messiah is a transliteration of the Hebrew word for king.

44

Longevity

Adam lived 930 years (Gen. 5:5): "So all the days that Adam lived were nine hundred and thirty years; and he had sons and daughters." Were the years Adam lived the same as the years in our time? Yes, they were the same. In the days of Adam they did not have the Gregorian calendar but the 930 years of Adam's life were the same as 930 years in our time.[99]

---

99 In chapter 48, "Resource," it is explained that God is the one who controls time. A year is determined by one rotation of the earth around the sun. Genesis 1:14 notes God made the lights in the firmament, in particular the moon and the sun, to calculate days and years. Adam, who was the keeper of Eden who walked and talked with the Creator, understood time. The years of Adam's life, which he himself tallied until his death, were the same as ours. If anything, they were more accurate. Augustine states the years were the same. He uses the month and days given in Genesis during the great deluge, the time of Noah, who the Bible presents as six hundred years old at the time of the flood, to demonstrate the patriarchs had a twelve-month calendar with thirty or more days in each month. Augustine, translated by Marcus Dods, *The Nicene and Post Nicene- fathers, St. Augustine, Volume II, The City of God.* (Ann Arbor, MI: Wm B. Eerdmans Publishing Company, 1979), 295.

The Mayans and Aztecs, Native Americans, had a 365-day calendar hundreds of years ago. Ancient people such as the Babylonians and Egyptians, like the Mayas and Aztecs, do not fit the evolutionary mold when one looks at their astronomical sophistication. The calendars of these peoples, while not as accurate as that of Adam's or our own following the modifications by the Julian and Gregorian calendars, obviously represent a historic linkage to earlier times, the time of Adam, when man was intellectually brilliant far beyond our comprehension.

One would have expected Adam's longevity to be much longer than ours. He was made perfect, which means his state of health was far superior to any human with whom any of us are familiar. Not only was Adam's health perfect, but he also had access to the Tree of Life, a fruit that had life-enhancing qualities, which must also have had long-term effects. In his early life, Adam was not subject to any aging process, for human death had not entered the garden prior to his disobedience in eating from the Tree of the Knowledge of Good and Evil.

One reason we don't know how old the earth is or how long Adam was on it, from a biblical perspective, is because Adam did not age until he ate of the forbidden fruit. We have no knowledge of how long Adam was on earth before he disobeyed God. This factor makes time before Adam's sin inconsequential.

I always thought Adam began the aging process when he disobeyed God. John Locke, in *The Reasonableness of Christianity*, thought the same. Locke wrote concerning Adam,

> He did eat, but in the day he did eat he did not actually die, but was turned out of paradise from the tree of life, and shut out for ever from it, 'lest he should take thereof and live for ever'. This shews that the state of immortality, of life without end, which he lost that very day that he eat (ate); his life began from thence to shorten and waste, and to have an end; and thence to his actual death, was but like the time of an end; and from thence to his actual death, was but like the time of a prisoner between the sentence passed and the execution which was in view and certain.[100]

Charles Phillips, *The Complete Illustrated History Aztec & Maya*. (New York: Metro Books, 2008), 12.

100 John Locke, edited by I. T. Ramsey, *The Reasonableness of Christianity*. (Stanford, CA: Stanford University Press, 1958), 26.

That Adam lived 930 years means the earth of his time was far different than the earth of our day. This is confirmed when we look at the ages of Adam's succeeding generations. Adam's son Seth lived 912 years (Gen. 5:8). The oldest man who ever lived on earth recorded in the Bible is Methuselah, the eighth generation from Adam. Methuselah lived 969 years (Gen. 5:27). Hence people use the phrase, often in a pun about another, commenting he's "as old as Methuselah" (a saying that is probably the oldest in history, being in use for over thousands of years). The youngest to die in the first ten generations from Adam was Lamech, who lived 777 years (Gen. 5:31). Enoch only lived 365 years on earth, and then God took him. Enoch did not die. He walked with God. For whatever reason, perhaps a prophetic purpose, God translated him or caught him away (Gen. 5:18–24).

Remember the first generations of humans on earth had Adam's DNA and obviously inherited his good health, which I think also accounts for their long lives. In addition, the climate of our earth was different until Noah, the tenth generation from Adam. Noah had never seen rain. In the days of Adam, "A mist went up from the earth and watered the whole face of the ground" (Gen. 2:6). God had not yet caused it to rain (Gen. 2:5). There was earth change in Adam's time. After he sinned, the ground began to have thorns and thistles (Gen. 3:18). But greater change came after the flood of Noah's day. However, the earth did not yet have the toxins, pollution, diseases, destructive insects, fungus, and assortments of weeds of our present day. These I think developed gradually, becoming worse and worse as time passed.

The main point, on the long ages of early earth dwellers, according to our resource, is the God factor. It was God who shortened mankind's span of life. God determined before He brought the flood in Noah's time to reduce the longevity of a man's life to 120 years (Gen. 6:3). This had do with man's wickedness (Gen. 6:5–6) and God reducing the span of time he has determined to give humans to respond by faith to the Spirit's work in bringing men and woman salvation through the Son of God, Jesus Christ (Gen. 6:3).

Nevertheless Shem, Noah's son (born before the flood), through whom we have the righteous line leading to Jesus, lived six hundred years (Gen. 11:10–11). Following Shem the length of men's lives began to decline. Arphaxad, Shem's son born two years after the flood, lived 438 years (Gen. 11:12–13). Abraham, ten generations after Noah, lived 175 years, which I take it was much longer than the average person (Gen. 25:7). Jacob, Abraham's grandson, lived 147 years (Gen. 47:28). Early, after Jacob had moved to Egypt where his son Joseph had risen to the second in power under Pharaoh, Jacob impressed Pharaoh with his age—Jacob being 130 years old (Gen. 47:7–10). Joseph lived to the age of 110 (Gen. 50:22). The Bible tells it like it is. Mankind went from living lives of great longevity to much shorter life spans.

God, in the time of Israel's kings, again shortened mankind's lifespan. In Psalm 90 the writer spoke of seventy years as a good old age. A long life would be someone who lived until the age of eighty.

> The days of our lives are seventy years; And if by reason of strength they are eighty years, Yet their boast is only labor and sorrow; For it is soon cut off, and we fly away. (Ps. 90:10)

Since atmospheric conditions in the time of Noah were altered, cosmic rays, due to a change in how the earth is watered, are not the same. As documented in the Bible, over time the life expectancy of people began to shorten. Mankind's bodies adapted to changing conditions. For example, remember more recently that Europeans were able to resist certain kinds of diseases; the same kind of afflictions, like measles, that devastated Native Americans, whose bodies had no immunity to such illness.

The ravages of war, famines, difficulties of farming, lack of knowledge on health care, man's inhumanity to man, various kinds of plagues and diseases, plus other factors took their toll all accounting for the shortening of human life on planet earth. Today chemical addictions, such as alcoholism, misuse of drugs, and smoking, shorten and take lives.

Presently cancer, heart disease, strokes, diabetes, Alzheimer's, as well as other types of illness, work against longer life expectancy. Stress brings body aliments that lead to early death. Various sexually transmitted diseases often lead to death.

There is concern about consuming the meat and milk coming from animals with unnatural hormone development (i.e., animals fed chemicals for greater business profits). Pesticides affect our crops adversely.

It seems like there's always some kind of a recall on a product due to salmonella. In spite of all this, *U.S. News and World Report* magazine in February 2010 developed an issue with the subject on how to live to age one hundred. They reported the average life span in the United States in 1900 was 47.3, but by 2000 it had lengthened to seventy-seven. By 2020 it is supposed to rise to 79.5. This, of course, is possible because of better health care, a better diet, and healthier lifestyles in individuals resulting from such things as routine exercise and the conscious practice designed to reduce stress.[101]

The same resource that reports Adam lived to 930 later informs us Joseph lived to 130. Then still later records that King David, thirty-three generations later, died old and advanced in years at the age of 70 (2 Sam. 5:4-5). Yes, it is reported Adam lived 930 years because Adam did live 930 years. My wife who works in geriatrics as a director of nursing had an elderly gentleman tell her, "Honey, them golden years, they aren't so golden." There were golden years. The great patriarchs of planet earth, beginning with Adam and his righteous progeny, lived the golden years. God gave them longer lives, and they also had better bodies, better diets, and a better atmosphere than we have. And for whatever reason, God determined (the God factor), according to his purpose and his providence, humans were to live shorter lives.

---

101 Deborah Kotz, *U.S. News and World Report, Volume 147, Number 2, Get Ready For the Age Wave.* (Washington D.C., U.S. World Report, Inc., February 2010), 19–22.

45

Giant

Adam was a giant. One of the ways to understand our resource, the Bible, is by comparing scriptural passages with other scriptural passages. The Bible gives us understanding of the Bible. Early in biblical history there were giants in the world. In the time of Noah, ten generations from Adam, we read, "There were giants (Nephilim) on the earth in those days" (Gen. 6:4). If there were giants on the earth, they were descended from Adam. The physical traits of the giants—that is, what made them giants—was determined by their DNA. Their DNA factor came from Adam. There were giants because Adam was a giant.

Someone might object, asking why the Bible doesn't record earlier that Adam was a giant. The answer is because the physical stature of Adam is not what is important. What was significant about Adam was his spirit. Adam, being the first man on earth, the son of God, was exceptional in every way. It is interesting and mentally stimulating to know Adam was a person of great physical height and ability. Adam and his immediate descendants would have been stellar athletes on any football, baseball, or basketball team.

The huge stature of people on earth relating to early beings is first referenced in Genesis 6:4: "There were Nephilim on the earth in those days." (NIV) Some say the giants were the result of fallen angelic beings called the sons of God mixing with the daughters of men (human beings). Others say the sons of God were the righteous line of Seth mixing with the descendants of Cain.

My thought is, why would God allow fallen angels to mix sexually with women who were human beings, the descendants of Adam and Eve? Fallen angels would be spirits, not flesh and blood. Why would such spirits be involved in the physical activity of sex? How could they do it unless they invaded the bodies of men and use the possessed bodies for carnal pleasure? Even so, how would that produce giants? The results of sexual union between men and women would still produce what is determined by the DNA of the possessed bodies. That is, possessed men would produce physical beings that were other physical beings like themselves, not giants.

Some who hold the theory that fallen angels produced giants (Nephilim) believe God destroyed the world with a great flood to destroy a corrupt race, a mixture of aliens and humans. The purity of mankind was preserved with the family of Noah, a righteous family. If that is true, how do we explain the presence of Nephilim, giants, in the time of Moses after the flood, centuries later? After Moses brought Israel out of Egypt, he sent men to spy out the land of Canaan. The spies reported Nephilim, were in the land "and we were like grasshoppers in our own sight, and so we were in their sight" (Num. 13:33 NIV).

The Bible informs us further about the Emim, giants. Moses instructed the Israelites not to go into the land of Moab, for the people there were descendants of Lot, the nephew of Abraham.

> The Emim had dwelt there in times past, a people as great and numerous and tall as the Anakim. They were regarded as giants, like the Anakim, but the Moabites call them Emim. (Deut. 2:10–11)

These people were not the offspring of fallen angels who had sex with humans. They were descendants of Adam.

Anak was a giant, the son of Arba, the founder of Kirjath-arba, later Hebron (Num. 13:31–33 NIV). The Israelites were familiar with giants, in particular the descendants of Anak. Five hundred years after Moses, giants were still in the land. David fought and killed a Philistine giant from Gath named Goliath who was six cubits and a span tall, a cubit being about eighteen inches and a span being six inches. Goliath was nine feet six inches tall (1 Sam. 17:4). There were other Philistine giants mentioned in 2 Samuel 21:15–22, one of them being the brother of Goliath (2 Sam. 21:19). It is referenced twice that these men, giants, were sons of the giant (verses 18 and 20). The giants were "born of the giant." The giant of course pertains to the race of giants. Who specifically, in that race, is the giant, the first one from which all giants descend? It's Adam! The point is there was a giant who had physical descendants who were giants. Giants descended from the first giant, Adam.

No one today is nine feet and six inches tall. Some people who are an abnormal size or height get that way through a tumor in the pituitary gland that causes gigantism. Usually this health problem involves other difficulties in the body precluding sports activities or physical functions that would make such size an advantage. The giants of the Bible were different. Goliath was a warrior trained in combat. My hypothesis is that the giants of the Bible inherited their size from the original human prototype, Adam.

Relating to stature, one of the most interesting accounts in the Old Testament on giants is the defeat of Og, king of Bashan, a disappearing breed. By the power of their God the Israelites defeated and killed him in battle. In summary we read in Deu.3:11:

> For only Og king of Bashan remained of the remnant of
> the giants. Indeed his bedstead was an iron bedstead. (Is
> it not in Rabbah of the people of Ammon?) Nine cubits
> is its length and four cubits its width, according to the
> standard cubit.

Og's bed was thirteen and a half feet long. He is called the last of the giants (in the area of Ammon). In other words, the giants, as a group, were gone. What about Goliath and the Philistines? The Philistines had giants, but the original giants were taller and larger.

Before leaving this subject, note there are various sources of information, outside the Bible indicating mankind was once taller. In *Undaunted Courage*, the story of the Lewis and Clark expedition, it is stated as late as the 1800s, President Jefferson was impressed by the gigantic size of the Osage Native Americans who visited Washington.[102] The Jamestown colonists, two centuries earlier, in the 1600s, report the Susquehannock Native Americans were seven feet tall.[103]

Much earlier, in the fifth century, Augustine wrote that some take exception to the length of years ascribed to antediluvians. Augustine of course went to great lengths to demonstrate the years subscribed to Adam were computed the same as years in his time, by the Julian calendar. Augustine went on to write,

> And so, too, they do not believe that the size of men's bodies was larger than now, though the most esteemed of their own poets, Virgil, asserts the same, when he speaks of the huge stone which had been fixed as a land-mark, and which a strong man of ancient times snatched up and fought, and ran and hurled and cast it 'scarce twelve strong men of later mold that weight could not on their necks uphold.' thus declaring his opinion that the earth then produced mightier men.[104]

---

102 Stephen E. Ambrose, *Undaunted Courage*. (New York: Ambrose-Tubbs, Inc., 1996), 342.

103 Grace Steele Woodward, *Pocahontas*. (Norman, OK: University of Oklahoma Press, 1969), 85.

104 Augustine, translated by Marcus Dods, *The Nicene and Post Nicene-Fathers, St. Augustine, Volume II, The City of God*. (Ann Arbor, MI: Wm B. Eerdmans Publishing Company, 1979), 291.

Augustine continued to write about times after the deluge.

> The large size of the primitive human body is often proven
> to the incredulous by the exposure of sepulchers … In
> which bones of incredible size have been found … The
> younger Pliny, a most learned man, maintains that the
> older the world becomes, the smaller will be the bod-
> ies of men … Homer in his poems often laments the
> same decline … As I said the bones which are from time
> to time discovered prove the size of the bodies of the
> ancients.

In this context Augustine wrote, "And if in the more recent times, how much more in the ages before the world-renowned flood."[105]

In another place, Augustine wrote that we were all in that one man, referring to Adam.[106] The giants in the world, those with photographic memories or superior intellect, or men with lives of great longevity all inherited what they have through the DNA of Adam.

Herodotus, who some call the father of history, in his writing reports a Spartan called Agathoergi who may have found the body of Orestes, the son of Agamemnon. The Spartan reported the coffin was seven cubits long. The man said "I had never believed that men were taller in the olden times than they are now, so I opened the coffin. The body inside was of the same length."[107] If a cubit was eighteen inches long, the body found would have been ten and a half feet tall.

Even in our time there is indication that early man may have been much greater in statue. On December 19, 2010, CBS's *60 Minutes* had a program

---

105 Ibid.

106 Ibid., 251.

107 Translated by George Rawlinson, *The History of Herodotus, Great Books of the Western World, Volume 6.* (Chicago: Encyclopedia Britannica, Inc., 1988), 15.

entitled *Superior Auto-Biographical Memory*.[108] They interviewed a group of people who could give great detail about whatever was asked in regard to any date of their lifetimes. Each person knew what day of the week a date was, like a Monday or Thursday, what the weather was like, and many particulars concerning that day. As an example, one man could recall the score of a baseball game, who did what, and many statistics about the game. Individuals in the group had phenomenal recall. Prior to their examination, they had no knowledge about what would be asked, and the information they gave was verified to be correct. It was found everyone in the group had an area in their brain that was greatly enlarged, an area not in normal use. When the area of enlargement was measured, it was determined if their bodies were enlarged according to the same percent as their brains, each person would have been over ten feet tall. If the same part of Adam's brain was the size as theirs or larger, he would have been over ten feet tall.

So what happened to the giants? Many of them, using their natural advantage in size as combatants, were killed. Others, and all of them through time, simply ceased to be.[109] How so, you ask? We know Adam's longevity was much longer than ours. The Bible records, through the years, that mankind's longevity shortened. Over time, as even Pliny and Homer observed about man's stature, it too declined, the same way mankind's longevity shortened.

---

108 *Superior Auto-biographical Memory.* (CBS, *Sixty Minutes*, 19 December, 2010).

109 As late as the time of Augustine in the fifth century AD, there were still remnants of giants from earlier times. Augustine referred to an incident in Rome where a giant woman overtopped invading Goths, an event, the way in which he referenced it, with which people in his time were well informed. "Was there not at Rome a few years ago, when the destruction of the city now accomplished by the Goths was drawing near, a woman, with her father and mother, who by her gigantic size over topped all others. Surprising crowds from all quarters came to see her, and that which struck them most was the circumstance that neither of her parents were quite up to the tallest ordinary stature." Augustine, translated by Marcus Dods, *The Nicene and Post Nicene-Fathers, St. Augustine, Volume II, City of God*. (Ann Arbor, MI: Wm. B. Eerdmans Publishing Company, 1979), 304.

46

The Son of God

Adam was "the son of God" (Luke 3:38). As noted, he was not born on earth but created on earth as a special being, perfect, the first man. Adam, before his fall, was without sin—a son of God, an earthling, called the son of God.

Adam was created to be a heavenly being. Heavenly beings, the sons of God, can space travel and traverse the heavens. God knew that Adam would sin. Nevertheless, Adam was created so that through Jesus Christ, he would have a resurrected body, a heavenly body that would dwell in heavenly realms (1 Cor. 15:45–49).

The Bible gives what is called progressive revelation. Adam and Eve were told that redemption would be provided to them through the prophecy recorded in Genesis 3:15. Jesus Christ is the promised Seed who would defeat Satan and bring Adam and Eve reconciliation to God. Additional knowledge given later is in Genesis 12:1–3. In verse 3 it is promised that all families of the earth would be blessed through Abraham (i.e., through his Seed, Jesus Christ). As time went on, more and more prophecy was delivered, honing down the message until Jesus Christ was born, lived a perfect life, died on the cross in our place, and was resurrected from the grave. Those who spiritually believe in Jesus as their Savior and King become members of the family of God—sons of God. The apostle

Paul wrote, "For you are all sons of God through faith in Jesus Christ" (Gal. 3:26).

Christians are called sons of God. The Scripture teaches people today who become Christians look back to the cross and through Jesus are sons of God by faith. Believers who followed the Word of God before the cross in the Old Testament covenant given by God to Moses at Mount Sinai—those from Adam to Noah and those from Noah to Moses, all who trusted in the Son of God by faith—are to be recognized as sons of God. When Moses wrote in Genesis 6:2 about the sons of God, he was writing about the righteous line of Adam through his son Seth.[110]

The Holy Spirit who guided Moses in his writing wanted to emphasize the concept of the son of God. In Genesis 5:1–3 it is stressed that Seth was made like Adam in the image of God. He and those who are of him are to be sons of God.

> This is the book of the genealogy of Adam in the day that God created man. He made him in the likeness of God. He created them male and female, and blessed them and called them Mankind in the day they were created. And Adam lived one hundred and thirty years, and begat a son in his own likeness, after his image, and named him Seth.

Even though knowledge about God's intention in Jesus Christ was progressive, Adam understood a great deal (read Isaiah 48:16-17). The Bible teaches Enoch, seven generations from Adam, before Noah and the flood, knew about the coming of Jesus and specifically the second coming of Jesus, including His judgment (Jude 14–15).

---

110 Augustine wrote that the sons of God in Genesis 6:2 were men, the descendants of Seth. In the City of God the people of God—sons of God—belong to the City of God, and those of Cain, daughters of men, are of the City of Man. "And by those two names (sons of God and daughters of men) the two cities are sufficiently distinguished." Augustine, translated by Marcus Dods, *The Nicene and Post Nicene-Fathers, St. Augustine, Volume II, City of God.* (Ann Arbor, MI: Wm. B. Eerdmans Publishing Company, 1979), 303.

> Now it came to pass, when men began to multiply on
> the face of the earth, and daughters were born to them,
> that the sons of God saw the daughters of men, that they
> were beautiful, and they took wives for themselves of all
> whom they chose. (Gen. 6:1–2)

The descendants of Seth, who were to live by faith, saw the descendants of Cain and intermarried with them. This has always been a problem for people who seek to live by faith. God had Moses warn Israel in Deuteronomy 7:3–4 about intermarrying with people who serve other gods. Those who seek to follow God go astray by intermarrying to others who serve false gods. This happened with Solomon, who married many foreign women and in his old age, was led away from his faith into the worship of idols (1 Kings 11:1–13). This is why Christians are warned in 2 Corinthians 6:14 not to be unequally yoked to unbelievers. Unbelievers will pressure people married to them, influencing them to depart from their Christian faith.[111]

> And the Lord said, "My Spirit shall not strive with man
> forever, for he is indeed flesh" yet his days shall be one
> hundred and twenty years. There were giants on the
> earth in those days, and also afterward when the sons of
> God came in to the daughters of men they bore children
> to them. These were the mighty men who were men of
> renown. (Gen. 6:3–4)

Nothing in Genesis 6:3 is communicated about fallen angels. This passage is about humans—not celestial spirits. Genesis 6:4 tells us there were giants on the earth in those days.[112] These were the descendants

---

111 Augustine identifies the sons of God as the righteous line from Seth. They got enamored with the daughters of men, descendants of Cain, and thus forsook God. "When they were captivated by the daughters of men, they adopted the manners of the earthly to win them as brides, and forsook the godly ways they followed in their own holy society." Ibid, 303.

112 Augustine notes there were giants on earth prior to the sons of God marrying the daughters of men. "Words of the divine book sufficiently indicate that already there were giants in the earth in those days in which the sons of God took wives

of Adam, fallen mankind, but giants, people of great stature, especially through the line of Seth, who preserved Adam's characteristics most perfectly.[113] After telling us there were giants on the earth, we read, "also afterward." Later, when the sons of God married the daughters of men, the result when they bore children was "mighty men who, of old, were men or renown." The giants on earth, first referenced, were not the result of marriages between the sons of God and the daughters of men. Mighty men, not bent on worshipping God, were the result of those marriages.

When the righteous line from Seth married those who had religious practices foreign to God, the consequence was men of renown who were like the gods we read about in myths, people who thought of themselves as immortal beings capable of superhuman feats. The offspring of these marriages, people of great intellect, longevity, and stature, were wicked beings, creatures of great might. Their lives were horrendously evil. Hence we have the next verse: "Then the Lord saw the wickedness of man was great in the earth, and that every intent of the thoughts of his heart was only evil continually" (Gen. 6:5). Going on:

> The Lord was sorry that He had made man on the earth, and He was grieved in His heart. So the Lord, said, I will destroy man whom I have created from the face of the earth both man and beast, creeping thing and birds of the air, for I am sorry that I have made them. But Noah found grace in the eyes of the Lord. (Gen. 6:6–8)

Warren W. Wiersbe, a well-known, outstanding teacher on the Scripture, in *Be Basic*, an Old Testament study on Genesis 1–11, gives us valuable insight on Genesis 6:1–7. Wiersbe wrote,

---

of the children of men, when they loved them because there were good, that is, fair." Ibid., 304.

113 Augustine calls to our attention the context of Genesis 6:4. The result of the sons of God marrying the daughters of man was that "the wickedness of man was great in the earth." Observe the focus is on man. Genesis 6:4–5 is about man not fallen angels, Ibid., 304.

Some interpreters view 6:1–7 as an invasion of fallen angels who cohabited with women and produced a race of giants, But as interesting as the theory is, it creates more problems than it solves, not the least of which is the union of sexless spirit beings with flesh and blood humans. Even if such unions did occur, could there be offspring and why would they be giants? And how did these giants (Nephilim, 'fallen ones') survive the flood (v.4; Num. 13:31-33), or was there a second invasion of angels after the flood?[114]

Even if fallen angels could make themselves appear in human bodies, why would they want to marry women and settle on earth? Certainly their wives and neighbors would detect something different about them and this would create problems. Furthermore, the emphasis in Genesis 6 is on the sin of man and not the rebellion of angels. The word 'man' is used nine times in verses 1-7, and God states clearly that the judgment was coming because of what humans had done. "And God saw that the wickedness of man was great on earth."[115]

Much about Augustine's view on this matter is included in numerous notes. His conviction is important not only because he is well recognized and a brilliant student of the Bible, but he is also an early church writer who gives us perspective from fifteen hundred years ago, the fifth century. Augustine informs us Genesis 6:1–12 is about men and not fallen angels.[116]

---

114 Warren W. Wiersbe, *Be Basic*. (Colorado Springs, CO: Chariot Victor Publishing, 1998), 88.

115 Ibid., 88–89.

116 Augustine, translated by Marcus Dods, *The Nicene and Post Nicene-Fathers, St. Augustine, Volume II, City of God*. (Ann Arbor, MI: Wm. B. Eerdmans Publishing Company, 1979), 304.

47

History

Adam is presented in the Bible as a real person in history. Jesus, in a document written by one of His disciples, Matthew, not that long ago in the scheme of things, spoke of Adam, not calling him by name but referencing his person. When some Pharisees, religious leaders of the Jews, questioned Jesus about whether a man could lawfully divorce his wife, Jesus replied,

> "Have you not read that He made them at the beginning male and female," and said, "For this reason a man shall leave his father and mother and be joined to his wife, and the two of them shall become one flesh. So then, they are no longer two but one flesh. Therefore what God has joined together, let not man separate" (Matt. 19:4–6)

Jesus referred to the beginning with Adam, the male, and Eve, the female. Jesus based His teaching on marriage from the written record on Adam and Eve in Genesis 2:24–25. Paul, when speaking in Athens, referred to Adam. He proclaimed,

> The God who made the world and everything in it is the Lord of heaven and earth … From one man he made

every nation of men, that they should inhabit the whole earth. (Acts 17:24, 26 NIV)

The apostle Paul referred to Adam by name five times in his letters, books of the New Testament. In 1 Corinthians 15:45, Paul wrote referring to Adam as the first living being. Human history begins with Adam. History is about people, not bones, rocks, or apes.[117] History has to do with writing. In the Bible we have a written record continuing through time that informs us about Adam. The record includes well-known people like Augustus Caesar, who reigned over Rome from 27 BC to AD 14 (Luke 2:2). The basic history of Rome and history since that time in the West is well known.[118]

Eve is recorded in two Scriptures in the New Testament. In 2 Corinthians 11:3 the apostle Paul notes the serpent beguiled Eve. We are not to be deceived by the Devil. In 1 Timothy 2:13, Paul mentions Adam was formed first and then Eve.

Jesus also spoke of Adam's son Abel as a real person (Matt. 23:35). Abel is referenced as the first righteous person who had his blood shed for the cause of the promised Seed. Abel is also mentioned twice by the writer of the book of Hebrews, in 11:4 as a righteous witness who still speaks about faith in the promised Seed and in 12:24 about Abel's offering of blood.

Cain is referenced by the writer of Hebrews in 11:4 as one whose offering was not pleasing to God. In 1 John 3:12 the apostle John notes Cain was

---

117 R. G. Collins' *The Idea of History* is a well-known book used in historiography classes to prepare students for a vocation in history. Collins wrote, "What kind of things does history find out? I answer ... Actions of human beings done in the past." It involves interpretation of evidence from documents. It is a science. It is for human self-knowledge. R.G. Collins, *The Idea of History*. (Oxford, England: Clarendon Press, 1946), 9–10.

118 We know a great deal about ancient Roman history, pre– and post–Jesus Christ. There are, as always, differing interpretations, but no one doubts the basics such as who the Roman emperors were. Note, for example, a list in *History's Timeline*. Jean Cooke, Ann Kramer, Theodore Rowland-Entwistle, *History's Timeline*. (Hong Kong: South China Printing Co., 1981), 229.

of the wicked one, Satan. Cain murdered his brother Abel. John instructs us that Cain murdered his brother because Cain's works were evil and his brother's works were righteous. Jude, the brother of Jesus, in his small letter, mentions Cain in verse 11, referring to "the way of Cain," which is an evil way, the way against God.

Adam and Seth are listed in Luke 3:38, the genealogy of Jesus Christ that goes from the first century AD back to the beginning, the first human. By the way, the writing just cited from the New Testament in the first century are more recent than the Gallic Wars written by Julius Caesar, wars having taken place from 58 to 51 BC. I can personally trace some of my family history back over five hundred years. A close relative of the 1600s could trace her family genealogy back over five hundred years to the ten hundreds. That's half of the time between now and when the New Testament was written. As noted earlier, in the scheme of things, the latter half of the first century was not that long ago, especially when some people tell us they can give us reliable information about data millions of years ago.

The history of Adam and Eve in the Bible, acknowledged by New Testament writers as fact, has direction. Not only did history have a beginning with Adam and Eve, but it is also linear—going somewhere. It began with the promise of a Redeemer, and it continues on until it documents His arrival, birth, life, ministry, teachings, miracles, death, resurrection, and ascension into heaven. History continues toward the Second Coming of the Anointed One, Jesus, and the beginning of a new earth with a new age for mankind.

History also has purpose. It revolves around God and specifically Jesus Christ. Man in Genesis began in a paradise. Paradise was lost. During the time encapsulated in history between Adam in the book of Genesis and the book of Revelation at the end of time mankind is to serve God, the Son of God. Those who are redeemed in the dispensations of that time span are seen in the book of Revelation as back in paradise but advanced beyond existence in the flesh, now as heavenly beings in the service of their King, Jesus.

History, understood from a biblical perspective, like all of God's creation, whether studied from the DNA in a cell, heavenly evening luminaries, fascinating animal life, the intricacy and beauty of plant life, or marvelous landscapes of many venues, is a most wonderful and masterful work of art orchestrated by almighty God. Visiting Disneyland or Disney World and experiencing the ride "It's a Small World After All" is an experience of immense enjoyment. The clothing of the various inhabitants in our small world, the different styles of houses and buildings—architecture, music, cuisine, diversified cultural peculiarities, as well as the similarities, in our world's people—is spell binding. It's God's world. He made it. He started it with two people. He beneficently has provided for it through the ages. He loved it then and loves it now.

There were ten generations from Adam to Noah. We don't know much about how people lived in the days of the patriarchs, from Adam to Noah, just like most of us don't know much about our own families four or five generations ago. From Noah to Abraham, there were ten more generations. In Abraham's day, the world was not very populated. In the Fertile Crescent and in Egypt there was civilization. As time went on, we read about Assyria, Babylon, Persia, Greece, and Rome. We know there were interesting cultures in China, Japan, India, Africa, and the Americas. People had spread out all over the world, were multiplying, and were trying to make life comfortable for themselves.

Time passed rapidly, always bringing change as God moved history toward His specific purpose in Jesus. There are heroic stories in man's journey, times of discovery, many different forms of artistic beauty, and to be sure great happiness in families that loved one another and lived out their lives well. But there was horror in war, the making of kingdoms, men who sought to advance their own status through the exploitation of others, and man's inhumanity to man as the Cains of our world served the wicked one. This is where we're at as we move toward a definitive end.

48

Resource

There is a resource that informs us about the creation, Adam and Eve, their children, Abel, Cain, and Seth, and the history of early mankind. The resource informs us about the first city called Enoch, which Cain built and named after his first son (Gen. 4:17). It tells us about Lamech, the fifth generation from Cain, who originated polygamy. Lamech had two wives, Adah and Zillah (Gen. 4:19). The resource references Jabal, the son of Adah, the father of those who dwelt in tents and had livestock (Gen. 4:20).[119] His brother was Jubal, who was the father of those who play the harp and flute (Gen. 4:21). Zillah bore Tubal-Cain, who was an instructor of craftsmanship in bronze and iron (Gen. 4:22).

The resource of which we write is called the Bible, the Word of God, or the Scripture. God our Creator gave us this perfect record to reveal His purpose for us.

God has also given us intelligent design in His creation, a marvelous demonstration of His presence and His supernatural intelligence. In his

---

119 Jabel, the son of Lamech, six generations from Cain (Gen. 4:20), was the father of those who lived in tents and had livestock. Many people, such as Abraham of Genesis 12, lived nomadic lives like Jabel. Living in tents was a preference. It did not come before living in houses, which Cain obviously had in the city of Enoch (Gen. 4:17). The Huns who contributed to the fall of Rome in AD 475 and the Mongols contemporary with them lived nomadic lives.

book *The Case for Faith* Lee, Strobel, interviewing Walter L. Bradley, an impressive scientist with a list of extraordinary credentials, was told by Bradley.

> What is encoded on the DNA inside every cell of every living creature is purely and simply written information ... Each cell in the human body contains more information than in all thirty volumes of the Encyclopaedia Britannica.[120]

When one studies this in depth, it becomes clear that natural selection as a mean through which life began is simply not true. The combinations it would take by natural selection to produce one living cell is not only mathematically improbable; it is impossible. Intelligent design substantiates the message of the Bible.

The genealogy of Genesis 5, the ten generations from Adam to Noah, the genealogy of Genesis 11 from Shem, Noah's son, to Abraham and the history of the line of Shem through the Bible to the genealogies of Jesus in Matthew 1 and Luke 3, are a phenomenal demonstration of God's documentation for His case presenting Jesus as the hope of the world. Most people don't know more than four to five generations of their genealogy. Here we have the genealogy of Adam from the beginning of the world to Jesus Christ, the Promised Seed the Redeemer of planet earth. The Scripture in this regard is totally unique. It is not what we find in myths.

A Scripture written almost two thousand years ago agrees perfectly with the second law of thermodynamics. The universe is decaying in terms of physical property in the process of entropy. We quoted in the last chapter Hebrews 1:11–12 that the earth and heavens are growing old like a garment and like a cloak will be folded up and changed. God will create a new heaven and a new earth. This scriptural reference in Hebrews is a

---

120 Lee Strobel, *The Case for Faith*. (Grand Rapids, MI: Zondervan, 2000), 109–10.

quote from Psalm 102:25–27, written by the prophet David under the inspiration of the Holy Spirit a thousand years earlier.

> Of old You laid the foundation of the earth, and the heavens are the work of Your hands. They will perish, but you will endure; yes like a garment; Like a cloak, You will change them, and they will be changed. But You are the same.

The prophet Isaiah through the Holy Spirit knew the world was not flat hundreds of years before the birth of Jesus. He wrote of the earth as a circle. In Isaiah 40:22 Isaiah wrote of God as "He Who sits above the circle of the earth."

The Bible teaches creation. God spoke the universe into existence ex-nihlo, out of nothing. God said, "Let there be light" and there was light (Gen. 1:3). So it was with all things in our universe throughout Genesis 1. "The worlds were framed by the word of God, so that things which are seen were not made of things which are visible" (Heb. 11:3). This is called by scientists today the big bang. Not everything has to have a beginning, but we know scientifically that everything that has a beginning has a cause. When we hear a big bang, we know there is a cause. The beginning or start of the universe requires a cause. The Scripture tells us that the cause was God. There is no other feasible explanation.[121]

God, who created the world, started time. It is easy to gloss over reality that positively proves God's control. The Scripture, affirming the creative action of God, records that God on the fourth day said, "Let there be lights in the firmament of the heavens to divide the day from the night, and let them be for signs and seasons, and for days and years" (Gen. 1:14). It's God who determines time. God is the one who makes a year a year. For the purpose of seasons, essential for success in agriculture, the solar calendar, calculated by one rotation of the earth around the sun, an exact

---

121 Ibid., 93–112.

year, is as it is. Man had continual problems computing how to keep track of time relative to a year until the Julian calendar and then the Gregorian calendar. Pope Gregory the XIII was fascinated with the calendar.

> Rome kept time on the inaccurate Julian calendar that had been in place since 46BC and was notoriously out of sync—he (Pope Gregory XIII) formed a committee that came up with the Gregorian Calendar, shaving six hours off the Julian system.[122]

The point being made here is that the calendar, while mathematically correlated by man, had to be adjusted accurately with the movement of the sun and the earth to get an accurate year, all set into motion and maintained providentially. No wonder Pope Gregory the XIII was fascinated by it. We all should be fascinated by it. The information on this subject in the Bible was written well over three thousand years ago.

It's also easy to pass over the significance of Genesis 5:5, where we are informed, "altogether, Adam lived 930 years, and then he died." (NIV) Adam, made in the image of God, amazing in intellect, traced the earth and its movement in relationship to the sun, knowing from year one how to compute time, recording accurately the years of his life. The years of Adam were the same as our own. Consider who he was, his perspective, and his amazing grasp of things. Adam's calendar was more correct than the 360-day calendar of the Jews in the time of Daniel. The very fact that the Scripture records Adam lived 930 years is phenomenal. Adam knew more about time than we do.

Lee Strobel in *The Case for Faith* quotes Norman Geisler, an outstanding Bible scholar, president of the Southern Evangelical Seminary in Charlotte, North Carolina, confirming the accuracy of the Bible as supported by archeology.

---

122 Alan Hall, *The History of the Papacy.* (San Diego, CA: PRC Publishing Ltd, 1998), 104.

There have been thousands—not hundreds—of archaeological finds in the Middle East that support the picture presented in the biblical record. There was a discovery not long ago confirming King David. The patriarchs—the narratives about Abraham, Isaac, and Jacob—were once considered legendary, but as more has become known these stories are increasingly corroborated.[123]

Strobel goes on in chapter 4 of his book entitled "Confirmation by Archaeology" to give specific examples.

In 2010 I read through the *New International Version Archaeological Study Bible*. I was amazed as I studied through the Bible at the many archeological excerpts on towns, people, and events referred to in the biblical text that are documented by factual finds through the science of archeology.

The Jewish faith traces its roots back to the Exodus from Egypt led by Moses under the direction of the God of Abraham, Isaac, and Jacob. The dates for Moses are about 1526 to 1406 BC. The internal witness of the Scripture is that Moses wrote the Law, the first five books of Bible, Genesis through Deuteronomy. "So Moses wrote down this law and gave it to the priests, the sons of Levi . . . and to all the elders of Israel" (Deut. 31:9 NIV).

The Bible presents itself as the Word of God, a written record of history to teach us about God and His plan for us in Jesus Christ. In regard to history, we are taught that Herodotus is the father of history. Herodotus, of course, wrote in the fifth century BC about the rise of the Persian Empire, its invasions of Greece, and the heroic fight of the Greeks against the Persians.[124] The history of Moses, however, is over nine hundred

---

123 Lee Strobel, *The Case for Faith*. (Grand Rapids, MI: Zondervan, 2000), 129.

124 Howard B. Wolman, *World Book Encyclopedia, H, Herodotus*. (Chicago: World Book, Inc., 2003), 213.

years earlier. It's God who began history, and it's God who gives us historical perspective. The first historian was Moses. Moses, by the way, received the best education of his day. "Moses was educated in all the wisdom of the Egyptians, and was powerful in speech and action" (Acts 7:22 NIV).

Moses wrote into Scripture what had been passed by word of mouth for centuries. It is possible written documents were available to Moses concerning Creation and Adam. The apostle Peter wrote that the prophetic Word, the Scripture, was confirmed, when he, James, and John saw Jesus, transfigured, illuminated as a brilliant light on a mountain shortly before His death on the cross.[125] Peter wrote in this same passage that no Scripture is of private interpretation. That is, it means what is written. He went on to testify that Scripture, prophecy, came directly from God through the Holy Spirit. "For prophecy never came by the will of man, but holy men of God spoke as they were moved by the Holy Spirit" (2 Peter 1:21).

---

125 Jesus is the Lord of History (Rev. 1:8). He began history with Adam, and He will end it, our present dispensation, with His second coming. Many historians today think of history as a science, and due to various and sundry influences, including those of nonbelieving philosophers, they teach anything that includes interaction with the supernatural is mythical. They make no distinction between the gods of mythology and the God of the Bible. Their preconceived philosophies circumvent any honest study of documentation given by God whereby His work and will are known. However, millennia after Adam, a mere two thousand years ago, five hundred years after Herodotus, Peter testified He saw Jesus Christ transformed (Matt. 17:1–7), and he saw Him crucified and resurrected (Acts 2:22–32).

Peter wrote these things are not cunningly devised fables (2 Peter 1:16). (They are history.) Peter argued the transfiguration proves the veracity of the prophetic word—that is, it confirms the Scriptures, our resource (2 Peter 1:19–20). Peter was a historic person whose testimony we ourselves can confirm in church history from well-documented sermons, writings, and artistic works by personages and dates in our own era back through time in Protestant, Roman Catholic, and Greek Orthodox records, as well as other groups, step by step, in a continuous flow, century by century, to the very life of Jesus Christ. Conversely, starting with Peter as a disciple of Jesus, coming forward in history, we see clearly the power of his testimony and truth about Jesus and the Scripture. The story in the Bible begins with Adam. He is relevant to every one of us.

Adam

The Bible, unlike some other books that were written by one person for a religious purpose, was written by forty people over a period of fifteen hundred years. All its books were written in a historical context. The Bible begins with Genesis, the beginning, and progresses with perfect unity to a definitive end, the book of Revelation.

Our resource contains significant and accurate information on Adam. The following is input from a speech by the apostle Paul at the Areopagus in Athens:

> The God who made the world and everything in it is the Lord of heaven and earth and does not live in temples built by hands. And he is not served by human hands, as if he needed anything, because he himself gives all men life and breath and everything else. From one man [Adam] he made every nation of men, that they should inhabit the whole earth; and he determined the times set for them and the exact place where they should live. God did this so that men would seek him and perhaps reach out for him and find him, though he is not far from each of us. For in him we live and move and have our being. As some of your poets have said, we are his offspring." (Acts 17:24–28 NIV) (In this Scripture the apostle Paul, in the first century AD, referred to one man, Adam, being the one from who all the inhabitants of the earth are descended.)

49

Prophecy

Prophecy is about the second man, the Second Adam, promised in Genesis 3:15. The Second Man, called "He," is "her Seed," the seed of Eve, woman, He who would bruise the serpent's head or destroy the work of Satan. The Lord God said to the serpent, the Devil, "*And* I will put enmity Between you and the woman, And between your seed and her Seed; He shall bruise your head, and you shall bruise his heel" (Gen. 3:15).

Prophecy is about Jesus Christ. In Revelation 19:10 we are taught, "The testimony of Jesus is the spirit of prophecy." The evidence or witness we have about Jesus as the Son of God, as the Anointed One, is the life and the significance of prophecy. Written prophecy is the Bible or Scripture. The apostle Peter, speaking of the prophetic word, taught,

> No prophecy of Scripture is of any private interpretation, for prophecy never came by the will of man, but holy men of God spoke as they were moved by the Holy Spirit. (2 Peter 1:20–21)

Adam received the first prophecy. It was about redemption to come through Jesus Christ. The same prophetic theme resonates through all the Scripture. The unity of the Bible concerning Jesus, the Son of God, must be emphasized and clearly understood.

Fulfilled prophecy clearly demonstrates the Bible's credibility.[126] Lee Strobel in *The Case for Faith*, interviewing the remarkable biblical scholar Norman Geisler, quotes him on that truth.

> The Bible is the only book in the world that has precise, specific predictions that were made hundreds of years in advance and that were literally fulfilled.[127]

Geisler reports,

> According to *Barton Payne's Encyclopedia of Biblical Prophecy*, there are 191 predictions in the Old Testament about the coming of Christ, including his ancestry, the city in which he was born, that he would be born of a virgin, precisely the time in history when he would die, and so on.[128]

In Micah 5:2, over six hundred years before the birth of Jesus, Micah prophesied that the Ruler in Israel would be born in Bethlehem. The scribes—people who studied Scripture—clearly understood this

---

126 Tim LaHaye in *Jesus* claims "fulfilled prophecy validates the Bible." Tim LaHaye, with David Minasian, *Jesus*. (Colorado Springs, CO: Published by David C. Cook, 2009), 43. It's critical to ascertain the credibility of the Scripture as a reliable document to know the historical Adam. Critics charge it is circular logic to claim the Scripture as a resource and to use the resource to support itself. Yet one cannot dismiss a testimony without seriously examining what it claims for itself. The Scripture itself claims divine inspiration for its writing. Furthermore it points to and leads to a historic figure—Jesus Christ. The existence of the universal church with its history and all its relating facets can only be understood through the factual existence of Jesus' death, burial, resurrection, and continued Lordship. Furthermore, that the Scripture was not written by one person at one time but many prophets over hundreds of years testifies to its truth. Prophecies were written and fulfilled in history. Scholarship can show that prophecies about Jesus written many years before His birth did historically occur, thus verifying the prophetic predictions about His birth, ministry, death, and resurrection.

127 Lee Strobel, *The Case for Faith*. (Grand Rapids, MI: Zondervan, 2000), 131.

128 Ibid. See J. Barton Payne, *Encyclopedia of Biblical Prophecy*. (Grand Rapids, MI: Baker Book House, 1980).

prophecy. When magi came to King Herod seeking the place of the coming Ruler's birth, the scribes' answer was Bethlehem (see Matt. 2:1–12).

The prophet David in Psalm 22 over nine hundred years before the birth of Jesus prophesied about the crucifixion of Jesus. Jesus, as the Son of God pre-incarnate, in this prophecy is actually speaking. In verse 16 He says, "They pierced My hands and My feet." In verse 18 He said of the Roman soldiers beneath the cross, "They divide My garments among them, And for my clothing they cast lots." (See Matt. 27:35.)

Psalm 22:1 starts out with, "My God, My God, why have You forsaken Me?"—a statement Jesus cried out while on the cross. (See Matt. 27:46.) Psalm 22:7–8 speaks of people who ridiculed Jesus while He was on the cross. Verse 8 contains some of the words people yelled at Jesus while He hung upon the cross: "He trusted in the Lord, let Him rescue Him; Let Him deliver Him, since He delights in Him." (See Matt. 27:43.) The whole Psalm is most amazing and even more spectacular when you realize verses 6 through 19 contain the very thoughts, feelings, and prayers of Jesus upon the cross, uttered by a prophet over nine hundred years before the event.

Isaiah, a prophet over six hundred years before Jesus, prophesied that Jesus would die for our sins. God put on Him the sins of the people who are to be redeemed (Isa. 53:5–6). Verse 11 indicates he would bear our iniquities. In verse 12, the prophet prophesied Jesus would be numbered with transgressors. And so He was—crucified between two robbers, counted as a criminal, killed with them. (See Mark 15:27–28.) Isaiah prophesied that Jesus would have a grave with the rich at his death (Isa. 53:9). Jesus was buried by a rich man, Joseph of Arimathea, who went to Pilate and requested the body of Jesus, burying Jesus in his tomb (Matt. 27:57–61).

David prophesied the resurrection of Jesus in Psalm 16:10. God said His Son would not be left in Sheol, the place of the dead. God's Holy One would not see corruption. The apostle Peter on the day of Pentecost said that verse did not refer to David because he was dead and buried, his tomb being there with them in Jerusalem. Peter said the prophecy was about Jesus, whom God raised from the dead. Peter said, "Of which we are all witnesses," speaking of himself and other apostles who saw Jesus crucified and also saw Him after He was raised from the dead (Acts 2:25–36).

There are many more prophecies, given hundreds of years before Jesus, that are about Him and those things that pertain to Him, proofs of Who Jesus is and what He is about, the things of God, beginning with Adam, and throughout our resource, the Scripture.

What I am about to do here is use the science of probability through prophecy to establish the case for the historicity of the life, death, and resurrection of Jesus Christ. In regard to probability, it is interesting to note this corollary, in a construct, in *The Case for Faith* by Lee Strobel. He cites Walter L. Bradley, who wrote *The Mysteries of Life's Origin*, in which he indicates that to get life, something like one hundred amino acids would have to come together in exactly the right process to create one molecule. It would take two hundred molecules in the right order in the right conditions to create a living one cell organism. All this would have to be programmed by a DNA molecule working with RNA directing the correct sequencing of amino acids. What would be the possibility of this happening by natural selection or random choice?

> If you took all the carbon in the universe and put it on the face of the earth, allowed it to chemically react at the most rapid rate possible, and left it for a billion years, the odds of creating just one functional protein molecule would be one chance in 10 with 60 zeroes after it.[129]

If you think about it, study it honestly on your own, you will realize that life on planet earth could never have originated by natural selection.

---

129 Ibid., 99–101.

Similarly, looking at all the prophecies concerning Jesus in the Scripture and having them fulfilled, without providential correlation, the hand of God, the true and living God, would also be improbable—impossible. Tim LaHaye, co-author of the popular *Left Behind* series, refers to Peter Stoner, chairman of the department of mathematics and astronomy at Pasadena City College in California before becoming professor emeritus of science at Westmont College. He stated that Stoner

> Calculated the mathematical probabilities of one man fulfilling a portion of the messianic prophecies and released his research results in a publication titled Science Speaks; Scientific Proof of the Accuracy of Prophecy and the Bible. Stoner concluded that the probability of one person fulfilling just eight messianic prophecies was I in 10 to the 17th power or 100, 000, 000, 000, 000, 000 to 1. He then calculated the odds of someone fulfilling 48 of these prophecies to be 1 to 10 to the 157th power.[130]

Prophecies about Jesus have been fulfilled, beginning in the time of Adam and throughout biblical history, foretelling specifics concerning His life, ministry, death, burial, and resurrection and the meaning of it all. Jesus taught that all things written in Scripture must be fulfilled (Luke 24:44). Jesus, after His resurrection, taught His disciples and apostles.

> These are the words which I spoke to you while I was still with you, that all things must be fulfilled which were written in the Law of Moses, and the Prophets, and the Psalms concerning Me.

---

130 Tim LaHaye with David Minasian, *Jesus*. (Colorado Springs, CO: David Cook, 2009), 65.

50

The Second Adam

Adam was the first man. Such a statement runs counter to mainstream thinking taught in our public schools and in collegiate academic instruction. For the most part, conversation on man's origin uses language that assumes humans descended from apes and early folk lived in caves. Nevertheless, Adam was the first man.

The genealogy of Adam, as all genealogy, is fascinating. Our parents come from two families, then four, then eight, then sixteen, then thirty-two, and on and on. I have been able to trace my family history back to over forty families for hundreds of years. It's amazing to know that you have sixteen great-great-grandparents. I have researched to know the names of each of mine, where they lived, and some things about them, and I wonder what they were doing at notable dates in history. We are limited in what we can find out. However, thanks to God, we can go all the way back to the beginning and know about the two people from whom we all descended.

Our great-grandfather all the way back was Adam. Thanks to our resource, there is much we know about Adam. What we know is quite significant. Knowing we come from Adam should give us a true identity about who we are. Furthermore, it tells us why we're here. It should bring us greater solidarity for peace. It also gives us dignity. In addition, it's the truth.

Adam was a human like us, flesh and blood, who lived in time on planet earth. We identify with Adam. Adam was one of us. Adam and Eve, his wife, had children. They worked for a living, were subject to the same passions as us, had to deal with tough situations, and died. The last words about Adam are, "And then he died" (Gen. 5:5 NIV).

Because Adam died, there is a Second Adam. Adam was not supposed to die. Adam was made to live forever, to be a celestial being, and created for glory.[131] It's the Second Adam who fulfills God's purpose to bring humans to glory.

> It was fitting for Him, for whom are all things and by whom are all things, in bringing many sons to glory to make the captain of their salvation perfect through suffering. (Heb. 2:10)

The first man was of the earth, made of dust; the second man is the Lord from heaven. (I Cor. 15:47) Adam was a created being, flesh and blood, made from the elements of the earth. Being the first man, the father of the human race, Adam, not having been born, was unique. The Second Man, Jesus, was born in Bethlehem, Judea, as a human. Though He was born as a man, He as the Son of God always was. *Adam was in the beginning. Jesus,* who existed before His incarnation, *made the beginning* (John 1:1–4, 14). Jesus is totally unique. He and He alone is fully God and fully man.

Adam is called "the son of God" (Luke 3:38 NIV). God made him perfect and put him in a paradise. He had a relationship with God. Though he

---

131 Jesus Christ brings His believer to glory. There are three stages of eternal life through which a believer passes. The first is justification, where one who believes having been forgiven through the blood of Jesus, is declared not guilty of sin by God, getting the gift of Christ's righteousness. The second is sanctification, where one living on earth is in the process of becoming more and more like Christ. The third is glorification, where the believer receives a glorified body like Jesus, a body that glows in splendor. The word *glory* in Greek, *doxa*, has numerous meanings. One is brightness or splendor. W.E. Vine, *An Expository Dictionary of New Testament Words.* (Nashville, TN: Royal Publishers, Inc., 1939), 483. Read 1 Corinthians 15:40–49.

lived on planet earth, he was a creature of the heavens. His Creator was Spirit, not flesh and blood. Adam knew God was transcendent, so he looked to the heavens. He didn't wonder if there was life out there. He knew there was life out there. He was made to be in the heavens as well as on earth. Thus he is called the son of God. But he was not a son of God like Jesus is the Son of God. Jesus is the Son of God because He is God. Jesus was always God. He said, "Before Abraham was born, I AM" (John 8:58 NIV). Jesus was "Emmanuel—God with us" (Matt. 1:23). Jesus is the Lord from heaven!

The First Man and "the Man"

Everyone should know Adam was the first man and that Jesus is "the Man." Peter in the first gospel sermon proclaimed Jesus as "a man." Like you and me, Jesus is a descendant of Adam (Luke 3:23–38). But Jesus is "the Man" because He is the root of Adam (and out of Adam), the pre-incarnate Creator. The Son of God became a man, Jesus, and is still a man. He is also "the Man" because He did what no other man could do. Peter in the first gospel sermon said,

> Men of Israel, hear these words; Jesus of Nazareth, a Man attested by God to you by miracles, wonders, and signs which God did through Him in your midst, as you your-selves know—Him being delivered by the determined pur-pose and foreknowledge of God, you have taken by lawless hands have crucified and put to death; whom God raised up, having loosed the pains of death, because it was not possible that He should be held by it. (Acts 2:22–24)

Adam was an impressive man, of great statue, a perfect being and thus exceedingly good looking. Jesus was ordinary looking. Judas, when he betrayed Jesus, leading soldiers to capture Him in the garden of Gethsemane, agreed to identify Jesus by going up to Him and kissing Him. Otherwise the soldiers might have gotten the wrong man. Isaiah prophesied that Jesus would have no beauty to attract us. Jesus was a man despised and rejected by His enemies. The man Jesus had sorrows and suffering (Isa. 53:2–3). We identify with Jesus. He became one of us. Truthfully, among all humans descending from Adam, only one, that is Jesus, is "the Man."

Jesus is "the Man" because His inner person was perfect. As the Son of God, when He became a man, He lost nothing of His divinity. (He temporarily gave up the glory He had with the Father before He came to planet earth.) The Son of God humbled Himself by becoming a man so He could die on the cross (Phil. 2:5–11). As a man Jesus had the mind of God. Jesus, as a man, since birth, grew in spirit, by the Spirit (Luke 2:40). Jesus is "the Spirit" by which we gain liberty (2 Cor. 3:17).

Adam's disobedience brought sin and judgment to all men – by one man's obedience grace came to reign through righteousness to eternal life. (Rom. 5:12) Adam's sin brought death into the world—death to the creation and death to every human being. Adam died spiritually on the day he sinned. Death, for a human being, is separation not only at the end of life but separation from God right now. People who do not have the gift of life by grace through faith (Eph. 2:8–10) are dead. They are not dying or are going to die. They are spiritually dead (Eph. 2:1–7). That is, they are estranged from God.

Jesus, as a man, never sinned, meaning He is qualified to save the world as well as individual men and women (2 Cor. 5:21). God taught Adam and Eve by clothing them with animal skins that they needed blood to take away their sin. They needed a vicarious act that would save them. And they needed to be clothed to take away their nakedness. The obedient righteous life of Jesus, given to us as righteousness when we accept Him by faith, makes us right with God. Jesus is the just one and the justifier, the one who is qualified to take away our sin and the one who died to take away our sin. Jesus reconciles us to God, not by what we do but by what He did for us on the cross (Rom. 3:21–26).

Since by man came death by man also comes the resurrection of the dead, for as in Adam all die, even so in Christ all shall be made alive.

(I Cor. 15:21-22) By a man, Adam, sin came into the world. Adam's rebellion turned the world over to Satan. Adam gave his headship over planet earth to the Devil. As the serpent bites man's heel, death, through war, greed, lust, murder, human diseases, natural disasters, and much more, has enslaved and tormented mankind since Adam's fall. Sin bringing death coming through the man Adam had to be removed by a man.

There was never a man who could bring deliverance to planet earth and mankind. The Second Adam, however, is someone, the only one who defeated Satan. Jesus, as noted, defeated Satan because He never sinned. Like Adam He was a perfect man. But unlike Adam, Jesus never knew immorality or imperfection. Jesus remained perfect throughout His life and through His death on the cross.

In addition, because Jesus was God as well as man, He takes away sin. Only God can take away sin. Satan put Jesus on the cross thinking that, as a man, he could break Him. But Jesus endured the cross without sin through the power of love (John 3:16). Jesus died as our substitute on the cross (Isa. 53:4–6). Our sin was placed on Him (2 Cor. 5:21). Our path to glory is through the life He gave for us on the cross. By the life Jesus gave for us on the cross, we are justified, declared not guilty of our sin by grace through faith (Eph. 2:8–10, Isa. 53:4–6, Rom. 3:21–26).

Jesus' victory over Satan and death is clearly demonstrated through His resurrection from the dead. He smashed the serpent's head.

> Inasmuch then as the children have partaken of flesh and blood, He Himself likewise shared in the same that through death He might destroy him who had the power of death, that is, the devil. (Heb. 2:14).

The first Adam became a living being. The last Adam became a life giving spirit . . . As we have born the image of the man of dust, we shall also bear the image of the heavenly man. (I Cor. 15:45-

49) Adam, made in the image of God, was supposed to populate the earth with a race made in God's image (Gen. 1:26–28). God wanted creatures, a special race of sons and daughters, for heaven. Adam, after sinning, however, began to populate the earth with beings in his own image (Gen. 5:3). Adam did the best he could. But he, as a sinful man in flesh, could not fulfill God's purpose. The spiral downward from Adam has been so great that today much of mankind has come to believe they are descended from apes. Not only does this not bring glory to God, but it will also cause many to be eternally damned. Such current mythology is earthly, sensual, devilish, hateful, dehumanizing, oafish, thankless, antinomian, rebellious, arrogant, and destructive.[132]

Jesus, the second man who is the Lord from heaven, the life-giving Spirit, did for us what the first man, a living being, Adam, could not do. Jesus gives those coming to Him by faith the forgiveness of sin, righteousness, and a new life. The new life begins with a spiritual birth (John 3:1–5), out of which emerges a new person (2 Cor. 5:17). Only those who have this new quality of life understand it. In truth, the Scripture, to be appreciated, must be understood from this new perspective. Those who would understand the things of God must do so spiritually (1 Cor. 2:10–14). Jesus transforms His people into the image of God, sons and daughters of glory, celestial beings. As we have borne the image of the man of dust, so we shall also bear the image of the heavenly man—that is Christ (Phil. 3:20–21).

The heavenly man ultimately, after the second coming of Jesus Christ, is a man who has a glorified body like Jesus Christ. The sons of God and

---

132 I noted when reading *The Crimes of Stalin* that Josef Stalin was in a seminary to become a priest because he wanted to help the poor. It was there that he read Darwin's *On the Origins of Species* and began to doubt the existence of God. Stalin's atheism led to the deaths of millions of people. Without a doubt, he is one of the worst humans ever descended from Adam, identified with the mark of Cain. He is one example of many that exemplify the destructiveness in the survival of the fittest philosophy, man from the apes. Nigel Cawthorne, *The Crimes of Stalin*. (London: Arcturus Publishing Limited, 2011), 8, 35.

daughters of God in heaven, like the angels, have indestructible bodies and are space travelers. The apostle Paul wrote,

> For our citizenship is in heaven, from which we also eagerly wait for the Savior, the Lord Jesus Christ, who will transform our lowly body that it may conform to His glorious body, according to the working by which He is able even to subdue all things to Himself. (Phil. 3:20–21)

For as in Adam all die, even so in Christ shall all be made alive . . . Those who are Christ's at His coming (I Cor. 15:22-23). Adam, who lived 930 years, brought death. He could not escape death. He died, and so does everyone. But Jesus Christ, who only lived for thirty-three years, brings life! How do we know this? Jesus gives us new life and eternal life by the power of His victory over death. The resurrection of Jesus demonstrates the reality of God. The resurrection validates who Jesus is and what He said. It gives credibility to our resource, the Scripture, and all it documents from Adam in the beginning through the life of Christ.

Lee Strobel in *The Case for the Resurrection* wrote, "For much of my life, I was an atheist. I determined at a young age that God didn't create people, but that people created God."[133] Strobel relates how he was unhappy with his life.

> My main value was to bring maximum pleasure to myself. As a result—and this is difficult for me to admit—I lived a very immoral, drunken, profane, narcissistic and even self-destructive life. I had a lot of anger inside me.[134]

When his wife became a Christian, Strobel saw she was making positive changes, so he went to church with her and was surprised by what he

---

133 Lee Strobel, *The Case for the Resurrection.* (Grand Rapids, MI: Zondervan, 2009), 9.

134 Ibid., 9.

heard. He decided as one who had much experience in journalism and a background in law to investigate the reality of the resurrection of Jesus.[135]

Strobel notes that Jesus claimed to be the Son of God (Mark 14:61-62). Strobel correctly determined:

> If the resurrection is false, then Christianity is refuted. But if it's true, then regardless of what any world religion teaches, Jesus is the one-and-only Son of God. And that changes everything.[136]

If Jesus came back from the dead, it does change everything. Strobel had used his belief in Darwinian evolution as an excuse not to believe in God. The resurrection of Jesus must be examined by any honest person relative to any philosophy or religious claim to determine what is the truth. Strobel became a Christian. His journalistic skills are now used to write superb books that are a testimony to his new belief and to the truth of "the Man," Jesus Christ.

Jesus, the Second Adam, gives new life to those who place their faith in Him. The presence of the Holy Spirit in the life of a believer is a guarantee that the things God promises will come true (Eph. 1:13–14). The Scripture that prophesied the Son of God's first coming teaches that Jesus will come again, removing the curse against creation that came as a result of Adam's sin. Christians will come with Him in resurrection bodies of glory (Rom. 8:18–23).

The apostle Peter, fifty days after the resurrection of Jesus Christ at the Feast of Pentecost, proclaimed that Jesus came back from the dead. He claimed he and many others who were present were witnesses of the resurrection. Peter used Scripture to teach the resurrection was fulfilled

---

135 Ibid., 10.

136 Ibid., 9–10.

prophecy. Peter concluded his remarks by declaring, "Therefore let all Israel be assured of this; God has made this Jesus, whom you crucified, both Lord and Christ" (Acts 2:36 NIV). Jesus is Lord—that is God. Jesus is also the Christ, King, actual Ruler of planet earth.

Jesus demonstrated He is our Ruler by walking on water, exercising authority over the wind and waves, causing the blind to see, enabling the lame to walk, cleansing lepers, healing all manner of diseases, casting out evil spirits, bringing people back from the dead, His teachings, His perfect life, His supreme sacrifice of love by which we are forgiven of our sin, and His coming back from the dead. His resurrection is the miracle of miracles and sign of signs, for all times, to bring people, the descendants of Adam, to belief (Matt. 12:38–40).

In Athens, Paul, in the midst of the Areopagus, preached about the Lord and His resurrection. Paul declared,

> Truly ... times of ignorance God overlooked, but now commands men everywhere to repent, because He has appointed a day on which He will judge the world in righteousness by the Man whom He has ordained. He has given assurance of this to all by raising Him from the dead. (Acts 17:30–31)

"The Man," Paul proclaimed, is Jesus, the Second Adam, who is coming to claim His planet and set up His kingship over our world.

The historicity of the man Jesus and His resurrection alone account for the beginning and existence of the church. The new birth and experience of God in the lives of Christians trumpets the reality of "the Man." Answered prayer of Christians documents the miracles and power of our Creator, "the Man." Those who study the Bible, our resource, the Scripture, know the credibility of the story of Adam and the providential care of our Creator, our Leader, our Spiritual Progenitor, the Second Adam, Jesus Christ, "the Man."

One doesn't need to have all the answers, to know everything to know something of critical importance. One doesn't have to know the why and wherefore of the dinosaurs to know there is a God, what He has done, what He is doing, and what He promises to do.

Adam was the first man. He was a type of Jesus. Jesus is the second man, the Second Adam, "the Man." Jesus is the way to God, to eternal life, abundant life, and celestial life. The faith of the apostles of Jesus (Acts 2:32), including the apostle Paul, was based on scientific empirical knowledge. They were personal witnesses of the resurrection of Jesus and would tell us with conviction and assurance that Jesus—the Jesus they personally knew—is the Son of the living God, the Second Adam who died on the cross to take away our sin. They would tell us that He was resurrected from the dead, that He now sits at the right hand of His Father in heaven, and that He is coming again. They would also tell us that the Bible, our resource for this book, is valid and credible, and we can believe what it has recorded about Adam. They would tell us that Adam was the first man. Indeed, *Adam was the first man!*

Index

Acknowledgments

A great number of people have influenced me positively and have contributed immeasurably to my life. I can't acknowledge everybody but will mention a few I believe moved me toward writing *Adam: You are Descended from Adam! What about Adam?* Thanks to each of the following:

E. R. Kerlin, my childhood mentor in the Kunkle United Methodist Church, Kunkle, Pennsylvania. He was not only a great man of God and an excellent Bible teacher but also a friend for whom I worked my junior year in high school. Edgar Hughes, my Dallas-area high school history teacher, was most excellent. Though him I acquired a love of history and learned to take notes.

Professor Robert Black at Johnson Bible College, Kimberly Heights, Tennessee, taught me how to study the Bible and instructed me through the Old Testament. Dr. David Eubanks, a PhD in history, the past president of Johnson Bible College (now Johnson University), a personal friend and superb teacher, continued to whet my appetite for history. Dr. Dean Walker, president of Milligan College, in two semester classes toward my history degree in that institution, taught a stimulating special seminar on the meaning of history.

Dr. Beauford Bryant, a graduate of both Princeton Theological Seminary and the University of Edinburgh at Emmanuel Christian Seminary, inspired me with his teaching on the New Testament, especially the book of John. Dr. Henry Webb continued to inspire me with the history of the church and utilized me as an instructor in his absence. Dr. Toyozo W. Nakarai, a renowned scholar in Hebrew, using his own book *Biblical*

Hebrew, took me through two semesters of Hebrew. Nakarai's instruction included the early chapters of Genesis using biblical Hebrew.

Dr. James I. Robertson, an eminent Civil War historian, the head of the History Department at Virginia Tech, befriended me. Here again I studied historiography. In numerous discussions with Dr. Robertson, a Christian and a member of the Episcopalian Church, he assured me he believed in the literal resurrection of Jesus Christ. Dr. Robertson greatly encouraged me.

Thanks to Dr. James Hess at South Dakota State University. His class on personality theories from his own book gave a clear view of psychology and its significance for understanding and helping us in human behavior.

Fuller Theological Seminary, highly academic yet true to the inspiration of the Scripture, greatly equipped me for understanding biblical truths and applying them to life. Writing a paradigm for an intimate marriage through a study of Genesis 2:23–25 disciplined me toward a more thorough knowledge of Adam and Eve.

I also thank my pastor, Kevin Key, at the Cornerstone Christian Church in Deltona, Florida, for his encouragement and the congregation for their prayers. Gratitude to Dr. Rich Love at the Cornerstone Church, who got his PhD under F. F. Bruce and worked on the staff of *Christianity Today*, for proofreading *Adam*.

A special thanks to my wife for the endless hours she spent listening to me about *Adam*. All praise to the Lord Jesus Christ, for whom I wrote *Adam* and to whom I dedicate this book.

Printed in the United States
By Bookmasters